BETTER HOMES AND GARDENS®

COUNTDOWN *to* CHRISTMAS

'TIS THE SEASON

BETTER HOMES AND GARDENS®

COUNTDOWN to CHRISTMAS

'TIS THE SEASON

CRAFTS EDITED BY KARIN STROM

RECIPES BY KATHY BLAKE

Better Homes and Gardens® Books

Des Moines, Iowa

Better Homes and Gardens®Books, an imprint of Meredith®Books:

President, Book Group: Joseph J. Ward
Vice President, Editorial Director: Elizabeth P. Rice
Executive Editor: Maryanne Bannon
Senior Editor: Carol Spier
Food Editor: Joyce Trollope
Associate Editor: Ruth Weadock

Countdown to Christmas: **'TIS THE SEASON**
was prepared and produced by
Michael Friedman Publishing Group, Inc.
15 West 26th Street
New York, New York 10010

Editor: Karla Olson
Production Editor: Loretta Mowat
Art Director: Jeff Batzli
Designer: Tanya Ross-Hughes
Photography Director: Christopher C. Bain
Illustrations: Roberta Frauwirth
Crafts Directions: Peggy Greig
Photography: Bill Milne

ISBN: 0-696-00049-0
Library of Congress Catalog Card Number: 93-080861

10 9 8 7 6 5 4 3 2 1

Printed and bound in China

Our seal assures you that every recipe in *Countdown to Christmas: 'TIS THE SEASON* has been tested in the Better Homes and Gardens®Test Kitchen. This means that each recipe is practical and reliable, and meets our high standards of taste appeal. We guarantee your satisfaction with this book for as long as you own it.

All of us at Better Homes and Gardens®Books are dedicated to offering you, our customer, the best books we can create. We are particularly concerned that all of our instructions for making projects are clear and accurate. Please address your correspondence to Customer Service, Meredith®Press, 150 East 52nd Street, New York, NY 10022.

If you would like to order additional copies of any of our books, call 1-800-678-2803 or check with your local bookstore.

ACKNOWLEDGMENTS

Karin Strom would like to acknowledge the following people: Peggy Greig, Roberta Frauwirth, all the talented crafts people who contributed, Karla Olson for her perseverance, Carol Spier for her patience, Chris Bain for his moral support, Joan Smith of Glen Ridge, New Jersey, and Valerie Simone of Blairstown, New Jersey, for use of their lovely homes during photography, and, of course, Colin, Viola, and Nadine for being there during a year of Christmas.

Kathy Blake would like to acknowledge the following people: Amelia Franklin, Gail Berry, and Laurie Middleton for help with testing and tasting, and Joyce Trollope and the Better Homes and Gardens® Test Kitchen for more testing and tasting.

Contents

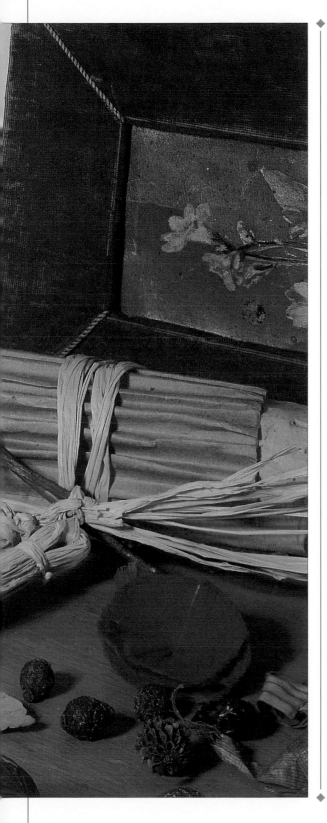

INTRODUCTION

If you're someone who loves to create a personal Christmas each year, baking delectable treats for guests and crafting delightful gifts and decorations by hand, you know that Christmas can be a hectic climax of celebration and gift-giving. In **Better Homes and Gardens**® *Countdown to Christmas* series, you'll find a step-by-step guide to the easiest and most memorable holiday season ever.

Although the holiday is almost upon us, there is still plenty of time to make this Christmas extra special. *Countdown to Christmas: 'Tis the Season* overflows with quick, last-minute gifts and decorating projects for the time when you're busiest. In it you'll find recipes for fabulous feasts and holiday entertaining, with menu suggestions that can (but don't have to) incorporate many of the foods you prepared from the pages of *Christmas On Its Way* and *Christmas 'Round the Corner*.

Even if you didn't get into them this year, the other *Countdown to Christmas* volumes offer wonderful ideas for years to come. *Christmas On Its Way* is filled with fantastic storable recipes—jams, jellies, spice mixes, and more—and exquisite gifts and accessories, each of heirloom quality, each a personal expression of appreciation and love. *Christmas 'Round the Corner* offers delicious recipes to freeze in anticipation of the holiday season, and charming, not-too-time-consuming gift ideas to craft ahead of time.

Better Homes and Gardens® *Countdown to Christmas* series is full of delicious Christmas recipes and great gift and decorating ideas. Each volume includes timely recipes and complete directions for crafts, and can be enjoyed on its own. Together, the books will really help you plan your holiday ahead and stay on track. If you wish, you can follow the suggestions for using foods you've prepared earlier or scraps left from your heirloom projects, but—even if you didn't have a chance to freeze your pie filling when the fruit was fresh or make the Pine Tree Quilt—you'll be able to complete any of the recipes or projects you wish.

There's no time like Christmas, with its warm well-wishing and gifts of love, enchanting decoration, and mouthwatering cuisine. There's plenty of time before Christmas for planning ahead—to make the most of the season as it arrives, so you can share in its joy and celebrate in style.

CHRISTMAS CRAFTS

PART

At
last! After
all the months of
planning and preparation,
Christmas is here! However,
there's still plenty of time to complete
the projects you've started, and there's even
time to create a few quick projects before Santa's
sleigh arrives. In fact, from wreaths to wrappings, there
are some things best left to the last minute. Many of the crafts
in *'Tis the Season* make use of materials you'll probably have around
the house, as well as fabrics, trims, and ribbons leftover from projects in
Better Homes and Gardens® *Christmas On Its Way* and *Christmas 'Round the
Corner*. And we've varied favorite motifs from some of the heirloom crafts, so if,
for example, you loved
the Pine Tree Quilt in
Christmas On Its Way,
you are certain to like
the Christmas Tree
Sweatshirt on page 58.

Home for the Holidays

THE CHRISTMAS SEASON IS FINALLY HERE, AND IT'S TIME TO FILL YOUR HOME WITH FESTIVITY, SONG, AND BEAUTIFUL HOLIDAY DECORATIONS. YOU STILL HAVE TIME TO CREATE A FEW FABULOUS DECORATIONS, SUCH AS CHRISTMAS WREATHS, GLORIOUS GARLANDS, AND ELEGANT HOLIDAY PLACE MATS.

CHRISTMAS WREATHS

Add a distinctive wreath to any room to spread the Christmas spirit throughout the house. Or consider giving a wreath as a holiday gift. The Small Wreath can be made as shown or covered with natural materials gathered on walks in woods and fields. For the bird watcher, make a charming Birdhouse Wreath. Gold-sprayed artificial ivy on a heart-shaped grapevine wreath makes an elegant and unusual front door wreath—and it looks fresh for many holiday seasons!

SIZES

- Small Wreath is 7" diameter. Heart-Shaped Wreath is 14" wide. Birdhouse Wreath is 15" diameter.

YOU WILL NEED

FOR ALL PROJECTS:
- 1 spool florist's wire
- Hot-glue gun and glue sticks

FOR SMALL WREATH:
- 6" straw wreath
- 1 pkg each dried rose hips, tiny pinecones, dried star anise, and assorted dried pods
- 9" length picot-edged satin ribbon, 5/8" wide

FOR HEART-SHAPED WREATH:
- Heart-shaped grapevine wreath base
- 1 pkg each artificial ivy and berries
- 3 yds green-and-gold wire-edged ribbon, 1½" wide
- Gold spray paint
- Newspapers, rubber gloves, and plastic wrap

FOR BIRDHOUSE WREATH:
- 2 bunches fragrant evergreen boughs
- 1 bunch each cedar berries, pepper berries, and grapevines
- 5 small toy wooden birdhouses
- Acrylic paints in assorted colors and small paintbrushes

DIRECTIONS

SMALL WREATH: Wrap florist's wire around straw wreath base for holding hanging loop. Fold a 9" length of ribbon in half and knot around florist's wire for hanging loop. Following photograph, position and glue assorted rose hips, pinecones, star anise, and pods onto wreath, covering as desired.

HEART-SHAPED WREATH: Cover work surface with newspapers and plastic wrap. Wear rubber gloves when working with spray paint. Work in a well-ventilated area. Lightly spray paint artificial ivy with gold. Let dry completely. Following photograph, arrange ivy and, using florist's wire, secure in place around wreath. Position berries and, using florist's wire, secure in place. Wrap ribbon around wreath and tie into a bow. Trim ends of ribbon.

BIRDHOUSE WREATH: Twist florist's wire together, forming a 15" ring base. Secure evergreen boughs to wire base with florist's wire, wrapping around entire ring to cover. Fill in spaces with grapevines, pepper berries, and cedar berries, securing with wire. Paint small birdhouses in desired colors and, following photograph, glue on as desired.

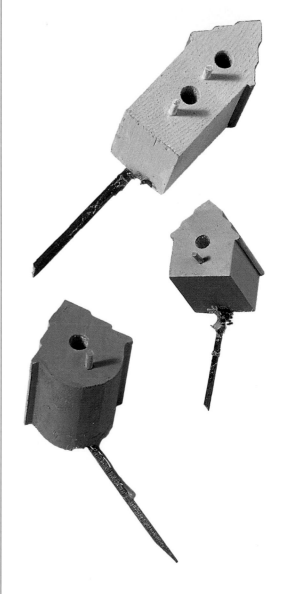

- *Birdhouse Wreath*

■ *Small Wreath (above); Heart-Shaped Wreath (right)*

GLORIOUS GARLANDS

Stringing garlands is one of the most versatile ways to decorate and needn't be limited to the tried-and-true popcorn-and-cranberries combination. A playful Pasta or Hard Candy Garland will liven up a child's room at Christmas. Colorful Ribbon or Metallic Pipe Cleaner Garlands are a perfect way to brighten any room. The Birch Bark Garland brings a touch of nature indoors. For those who travel during the holidays and don't want the hassel of decorating a whole tree, several garlands festooning the living room provide a perfect solution.

SIZE

- Each garland is approximately 6' long.

YOU WILL NEED

FOR PASTA GARLAND:
- 1 box each rigatoni and pasta wheels pasta
- 2 yds red twisted cording, 1/8" diameter
- Small spray cans glossy enamel in red, green, purple, and gold
- Newspapers, rubber gloves, and plastic wrap

FOR RIBBON GARLAND:
- 4 yds striped ribbon in burgundy, hunter green, and gold, 7/8" wide
- Hot-glue gun and glue sticks
- Scissors and ruler

FOR METALLIC PIPE CLEANER GARLAND:
- 45 to 60 assorted metallic pipe cleaners, each 12" long
- Scissors and ruler

FOR HARD CANDY GARLAND:
- Bags of assorted colored-cellophane twisted and wrapped candy
- Mini stapler and staples

FOR BIRCH BARK GARLAND:
- Pieces of birch bark (see page 22, "Nature Note")
- 2 yds red-and-green twisted cording, 1/8" diameter
- Scissors and pencil
- Tracing paper

DIRECTIONS

PASTA GARLAND: Cover work surface with newspapers and plastic wrap. Wear rubber gloves when working with spray paint. Work in a well-ventilated area. One at a time, spray paint both sides of approximately 100 (or desired amount) pieces of rigatoni gold. Spray paint both sides of 35 pasta wheels in each of the remaining three colors. Let paints dry completely. Following photograph, string pasta on cording, alternating colors and shapes as desired. Tie a large knot at each end to secure.

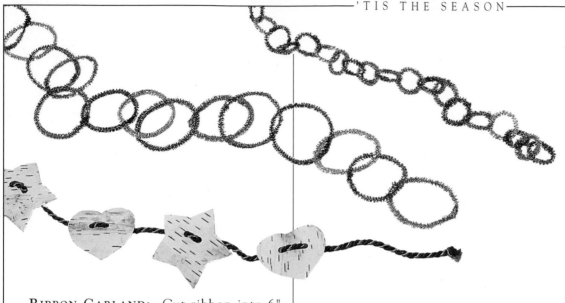

HARD CANDY GARLAND: Following photograph, staple twisted ends of cellophane wrapping together. Alternate colors as desired.

BIRCH BARK GARLAND: Using patterns below, trace approximately 16 small heart and star patterns onto tracing paper, then onto birch bark. Cut out. Using scissors, poke two holes through the center of each shape as indicated. Following photograph, thread shapes on twisted cording, alternating shapes and leaving 1½" to 2" between each shape.

RIBBON GARLAND: Cut ribbon into 6" lengths. Form a loop with one piece, overlapping and gluing ends. Following photograph, fold second length in same manner, interlocking with first loop, to make a ribbon chain. Continue until garland is desired length.

METALLIC PIPE CLEANER GARLAND: Cut pipe cleaners into 8" pieces (save the remaining 4" piece from each pipe cleaner to make a smaller loop garland). Form a loop with one piece, twisting the ends together to secure, then pushing them flat against loop. Following photograph, interlock each new loop with the one just made to form a chain. Alternate colors as desired.

NATURE NOTE

When collecting birch bark for the Glorious Garlands (page 21) and the Nature Ornaments (page 28), do not pull the bark off the tree, as this will harm the tree. Instead, collect pieces that have fallen to the ground.

▪ *Small Heart and Star Patterns for Birch Bark Garland (actual size)*

Quick and Beautiful Ornaments

In olden times, Christmas tree ornaments were made from found objects—fabric scraps saved from favorite clothing, materials gathered from nature. Later, glass balls became the most sought-after decorations to hang on the holiday evergreen tree. Our collection of ornaments offers a sampling of each type—and they can all be made at almost the very last moment! The Victorian Moiré Ornaments make use of fabric scraps. Purchased glass balls are decorated to make the elegant Gold Star Ornaments. The Nature Ornaments are all made from natural ingredients (although city dwellers may want to purchase materials in a crafts shop).

VICTORIAN MOIRÉ ORNAMENTS

SIZES

- Ornaments are approximately 3" to 4".

YOU WILL NEED

- 2 foam balls for large ornaments, 3½" diameter
- 1 foam ball for small ornament, 2½" diameter
- ¼ yd each moiré fabric in pink, purple, and white
- 1 yd each satin cording in dark red and dark green, ½" diameter
- 1¼ yds lightweight satin cording in ivory, ¼" diameter
- 1 each dark red and dark green 3½" tassels

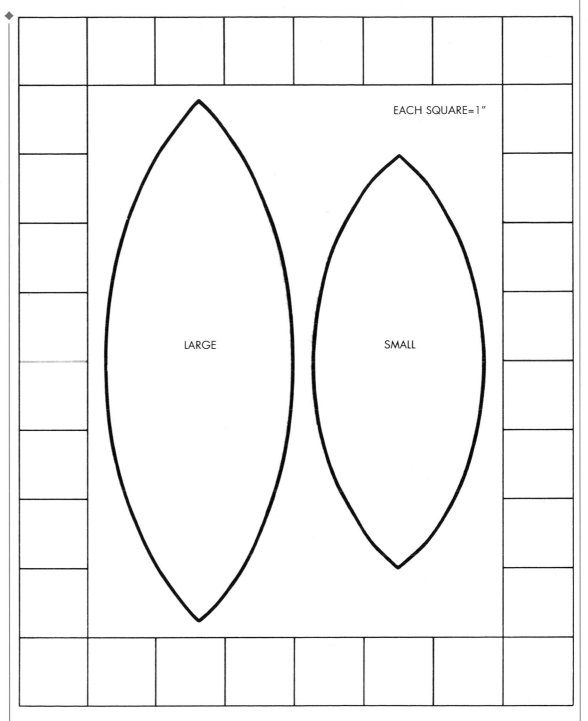

EACH SQUARE=1"

LARGE

SMALL

- *Victorian Moiré Ornaments Patterns*

- 1 ivory 2½" tassel
- Sharp-pointed scissors and felt pen
- Hot-glue gun and glue sticks

DIRECTIONS

FOR EACH ORNAMENT: Enlarge pattern on page 23 (see below, "Enlarging Patterns") and, following photograph, cut out four pieces of moiré fabric for each ornament. Using the felt pen, evenly divide foam ball into four sections. Beginning at middle of one section, place glue on lines. Place middle of one edge of one piece of fabric in glue and pinch edge up into gathers, pressing into glue. Repeat on other edge. Continue working up lines to point, trimming excess fabric at ends as needed. Repeat on opposite side of ball. Using the same method but placing the glue on fabric, glue remaining sections so edges overlap. Glue cording over seams, forming a loop at the top for hanging. Glue tassel to bottom of ornament. For small ornament, tie a 3½" bow of ivory cording and glue in place. Tie ends in a knot and trim. For each large ornament, tie a 6" bow of cording and glue in place. Tie ends in a knot and trim.

ENLARGING PATTERNS

With ruler and pencil, extend the grid lines over the diagram. On paper, draw a grid of squares in the size indicated by the scale given with the diagram, being sure your grid has the same number of rows and columns of squares as the original. Refer to the diagram and mark the full-size grid where the pattern lines intersect with the grid lines. Connect the markings. Refine any details if necessary.

GOLD STAR ORNAMENTS

SIZES

- Ornaments are 3" to 4".

YOU WILL NEED

- 2 frosted glass ornaments, 3" diameter
- 1 frosted glass ornament, 4" diameter
- 1 pkg gold self-adhesive stars, ⅝" wide
- 1 yd each gold ribbons, ⅛" wide, ⅝" wide, and 11/16" wide
- 4 small gold star charms
- 2 large gold star charms
- Sharp-pointed scissors and yellow thread
- Hot-glue gun and glue sticks

DIRECTIONS

FOR EACH ORNAMENT: Remove ornament wires from ornament.

SMALL STAR CHARM ORNAMENT: Following photograph and using ⅛" wide ribbon, divide ornament in half by wrapping and gluing ribbon around ball, starting and ending at the top, leaving top wire hole exposed. Glue in place. Repeat on opposite side of ornament to divide ornament into quarters. Cut two pieces of ribbon, each 15" long. Tie each into a bow. Fold ends of ribbon in to form a point. Slipstitch ends closed and, following photograph, tack small star charms in place with yellow thread. Clip loops of bow open with diagonal cuts. Place small dots of glue on ribbons at knot and press together to form a tassel. Glue tassel to bottom of ornament. Peel and stick stars to ball, using three per section. Replace wire in ornament.

SMALL ORNAMENT WITH BOW: Following photograph and using ⅝" wide ribbon, divide ornament in half by wrapping and gluing ribbon around center of ball. Peel and stick stars to ornament. Tie remaining ribbon into 4" bow through wire loop. Trim ends of ribbon in inverted "V" shape. Replace wire in ornament.

LARGE STAR CHARM ORNAMENT: Following photograph and using 11/16" wide ribbon, divide ornament in half by wrapping and gluing ribbon around ball, starting and ending at top, leaving top wire hole exposed. Tie remaining ribbon into 5" bow through wire loop. Trim one end of bow to 5½" and the other to 4½". Fold ends in to form a point. Slipstitch ends closed and, following photograph, tack large charms in place. Peel and stick stars to ball. Replace wire in ornament.

- *Victorian Moiré Ornaments (left)*

■ *Gold Star Ornaments (left); Nature Ornaments (above)*

NATURE ORNAMENTS

SIZES

- Ornaments are 3" to 7".

YOU WILL NEED

FOR WHITE TWIG ORNAMENT:

- 35 to 50 small twigs, each approximately ⅛" thick and 7" long
- White spray paint
- Thin wire
- Newspapers and plastic wrap

FOR GOLD TWIG STAR ORNAMENT:

- 5 twigs, each approximately ¼" thick and 7" long
- Gold spray paint
- Hot-glue gun and glue sticks
- 6" length gold cording, ⅛" diameter
- Newspapers and plastic wrap

FOR WHITE-AND-GOLD TWIG ORNAMENT:

- 8 to 10 small twigs, each approximately ¼" thick and 7" long
- White spray paint
- 2 oz squeeze bottle gold acrylic paint
- Natural sponge
- 12" length gold-and-white cording, ⅛" diameter
- Hot-glue gun and glue sticks
- Newspapers and plastic wrap

FOR HEART ORNAMENT:

- 5" square plywood, ⅛" thick
- Pieces of birch bark (see page 22, "Nature Note")
- Assorted dried mosses, flowers, lichens, and tiny pinecones
- 2 small twigs, each approximately ⅛" thick and 6" long

- *Heart Ornament Pattern (actual size)(above)*

- 6" length gold cording, ⅛" diameter
- Craft knife, craft glue, and pencil
- Jigsaw and drill
- Tracing paper

FOR STAR ORNAMENT:

- 5" square plywood, ⅛" thick
- Dried sheet moss, rose, chrysanthemums, and larkspurs
- 10 small twigs, each approximately ⅛" thick and 3" long
- 12" length wire-edged ombré ribbon, 1" wide
- Craft knife, craft glue, pencil, and jigsaw

- *Nature Ornaments (right)*

FOR HEART WREATH ORNAMENT #1:

- 5" wide wooden heart-shaped wreath
- Dried sheet moss, strawflowers, statice, and larkspur
- 6" length gold string
- Craft glue

FOR HEART WREATH ORNAMENT #2:

- 5" wide wooden heart-shaped wreath
- Dried globe amaranth and lavender stems
- 12" length wired-edged ombré ribbon, 1" wide
- Craft glue

FOR LAVENDER BALL ORNAMENT:
- 2" foam ball
- Dried lavender flowers, berries, and sprigs
- 12" length wire-edged ombré ribbon, 1" wide
- Craft glue

FOR FLORAL BALL ORNAMENT:
- 2" foam ball
- Assorted dried strawflowers, chrysanthemums, and larkspur
- 12" length wire-edged ombré ribbon, 1" wide
- Hot-glue gun and glue sticks

DIRECTIONS

NOTE: Cover work surface with newspapers and plastic wrap. Wear rubber gloves when working with spray paint. Work in a well-ventilated area.

WHITE TWIG ORNAMENT: Following photograph, arrange and overlap twigs in a circular motif. Wire together at center. Fold a piece of wire in half and tie to one point for hanging loop. Spray ornament with white paint, covering entire surface.

GOLD TWIG STAR ORNAMENT: Following photograph, arrange and glue twigs in a five-pointed star motif. Fold gold cording in half and glue to one point for hanging loop. Spray ornament with gold paint, covering entire surface.

WHITE-AND-GOLD TWIG ORNAMENT: Following photograph, arrange and glue twigs in a circular motif. Spray ornament with white paint, covering entire surface. Let dry completely. Sponge paint with gold paint. Fold cording in half and glue to one point for hanging loop.

HEART ORNAMENT: Using pattern on page 28, trace one heart onto plywood and two onto birch bark. Cut out. Glue a birch bark heart on each side of the plywood heart. Drill a small hole at middle of top of heart for hanging loop. Following photograph, arrange and glue assorted dried mosses, flowers, lichens, and pinecones on front of heart. Glue twigs around sides of heart, covering plywood. Thread gold cording through hole and knot for hanging loop.

Star Ornament Pattern (actual size)

STAR ORNAMENT: Using pattern above, trace one star onto plywood. Cut out. Cover both sides with craft glue, one at a time, and attach moss. Cut twigs to same size of side of each point and glue in place. Following photograph, glue flowers at each point and center of star. Fold ribbon in half and glue to one point for hanging loop, allowing 3" ends for streamers. Trim ends of ribbon.

HEART WREATH ORNAMENT #1:
Cover both sides of heart wreath with craft glue, one at a time, and attach moss, covering completely. Following photograph, glue flowers in place on front. Fold and knot gold string and glue in place at middle of top of heart for hanging loop.

HEART WREATH ORNAMENT #2:
Following photograph, center and glue globe amaranth in place on front of wreath. Cover and glue lavender stems in place on sides until entire wreath is covered. Fold ribbon and glue in place at middle of top of heart for hanging loop.

LAVENDER BALL ORNAMENT:
Cover surface of foam ball with glue. Roll in lavender flowers to completely cover. Fold ribbon in half and glue in place at top of ball, allowing 3" ends for streamers. Trim ends of ribbon. Following photograph, glue sprigs and berries around hanging loop.

FLORAL BALL ORNAMENT:
Following photograph, cover surface of foam ball with flowers using hot-glue gun. Fold ribbon in half and glue in place at top of ball, allowing 3" ends for streamers. Trim ends of ribbon.

CANDLELIGHT COLLECTION

Light up your home this holiday season. Candlelight creates a magical effect, especially when candles are grouped together. Our collection includes a charming Spice Candle Holder, a cozy Votive Candle Caddie, a fragrant painted Citronella Pot Candle (citronella candles are available at most garden shops year-round), and a gold-studded Dressed-Up Candle. Or consider giving a gift of Wrapped Candles—always a welcome present.

SIZES

- Spice Candle Holder is 4" high. Votive Candle Caddie is 5" x 5" x 2" high. Citronella Pot Candle is 6" high. Dressed-Up Candle is 7" high. Wrapped Candles are 9" long.

YOU WILL NEED

FOR SPICE CANDLE HOLDER:
- 4" clay flowerpot
- 1 pkg each dried miniature roses, pinecones, whole cloves, whole bay leaves, and assorted pods
- Hot-glue gun and glue sticks
- 3" candle

FOR VOTIVE CANDLE CADDIE:
- 9 votive candles
- 5" square plywood, ⅛" thick
- 2 oz squeeze bottle red acrylic paint
- 4 birch twigs, each approximately ¼" thick and 2" long
- 8 birch twigs, each approximately ¼" thick and 5" long
- Pruning shears and paintbrush
- Drill and brown panel nails

FOR CITRONELLA POT CANDLE:
- 6" citronella candle in galvanized tin pot
- 2 oz squeeze bottles acrylic paint in blue and ocher
- Crackle paint
- Paintbrush

FOR DRESSED-UP CANDLE:
- 7" white pillar candle
- 1 pkg brass studs

FOR WRAPPED CANDLES:
- Five taper candles, 9" long
- 6" x 12" piece handmade paper
- 4" x 8" piece corrugated paper
- Small amount gold leaf accent
- Strip of raffia
- 2 each raffia tassels and small twigs

DIRECTIONS

SPICE CANDLE HOLDER: Following photograph, position and glue whole bay leaves around base of flowerpot, overlapping leaves and completely covering area. Arrange and glue miniature roses, cloves, tiny pinecones, and pods on rim, completely covering area. Set candle in holder.

VOTIVE CANDLE CADDIE: Paint plywood with red paint. Let dry completely. Drill one hole ½" from one end of each 2" twig post. On two of the twigs, drill a second hole ⅛" higher and a quarter turn to the right of the first hole; on the other two twigs, drill a second hole ⅛" higher and a quarter turn to the left of the first hole. Drill holes in each corner of plywood for nails for twig posts. Nail twig posts from bottom of plywood into each corner. Position and nail rails into each twig post. Arrange one twig on each side of plywood base and drill and nail in place. Arrange candles in caddie.

CITRONELLA POT CANDLE: Paint top third of galvanized tin container with ocher, the middle third with blue, and the last third with ocher. Let dry completely. Following manufacturer's instructions, apply crackle paint. Let dry completely. Paint again alternating colors to allow opposite color to show through underneath.

DRESSED-UP CANDLE: Following photograph, press brass studs into candle as desired.

WRAPPED CANDLES: Arrange five candles in a bundle. Wrap with handmade paper, then wrap again with corrugated paper. Position gold leaf accent, raffia tassels, and twigs. Tie with raffia to secure.

MINI STOCKINGS

Darling, fun-to-make little stockings are certain to be favorites of the smaller family members. Decorate bedposts, the mantel in the family room, or a stairway with a group of Mini Stockings. They provide an ideal use for the fabric, ribbon, and trim scraps you've been saving, and this is a great project for kids.

SIZE

- Each stocking is 7" tall.

YOU WILL NEED

FOR EACH STOCKING:
- 10" square red felt
- Matching thread and dressmaker's carbon
- Scissors and pencil
- Craft glue

FOR LACE AND BUTTON STOCKING:
- 10" square red felt
- 1 yd red polka dot ribbon, 1" wide
- 6" length red polka dot ribbon, 3/8" wide
- 1 yd white lace edging, 1/2" wide
- Scraps of white narrow lace and ribbons
- 15 assorted white pearl buttons
- Red embroidery floss

FOR HOLLY STOCKING:
- 10" square each in green and white felt
- 3 medium acrylic red jewels
- 6" length red ribbon, 1/2" wide
- 2 oz squeeze bottle green glitter paint
- Pinking shears

FOR HEART STOCKING:
- 10" square white felt
- Green embroidery floss
- 6" length green ribbon, 1/2" wide

- 12" length green ribbon, 1" wide
- Pinking shears

FOR GLITTER STOCKING:
- 10" square each green and white felt
- 6 acrylic silver star jewels
- 4 assorted large and medium red acrylic jewels
- 6" length red ribbon, 1/2" wide
- 2 oz squeeze bottles glitter paint in green and clear
- Pinking shears and paintbrush

DIRECTIONS

LACE AND BUTTON STOCKING: Enlarge pattern on page 36 (see page 25, "Enlarging Patterns") for large stocking and trace two onto red felt. Cut out. Place together, aligning edges, and topstitch, leaving top edge open. Transfer lace lines to stocking front using dressmaker's carbon. Glue scraps of lace and ribbon along lace lines, overlapping raw ends. Following photograph, glue assorted buttons in place. Cut one 9½" piece of 1" wide ribbon and two 9½" pieces of ½" wide lace edging. Stitch lace edging onto each long edge of ribbon for cuff. With wrong side of cuff against right side of stocking, glue cuff to top edge of stocking, wrapping around stocking and overlapping at center of back. Fold 6" piece of polka-dot ribbon in half and glue at top corner for hanging loop. Tie bow with remaining wide ribbon and glue at hanging loop. Trim ends of ribbon.

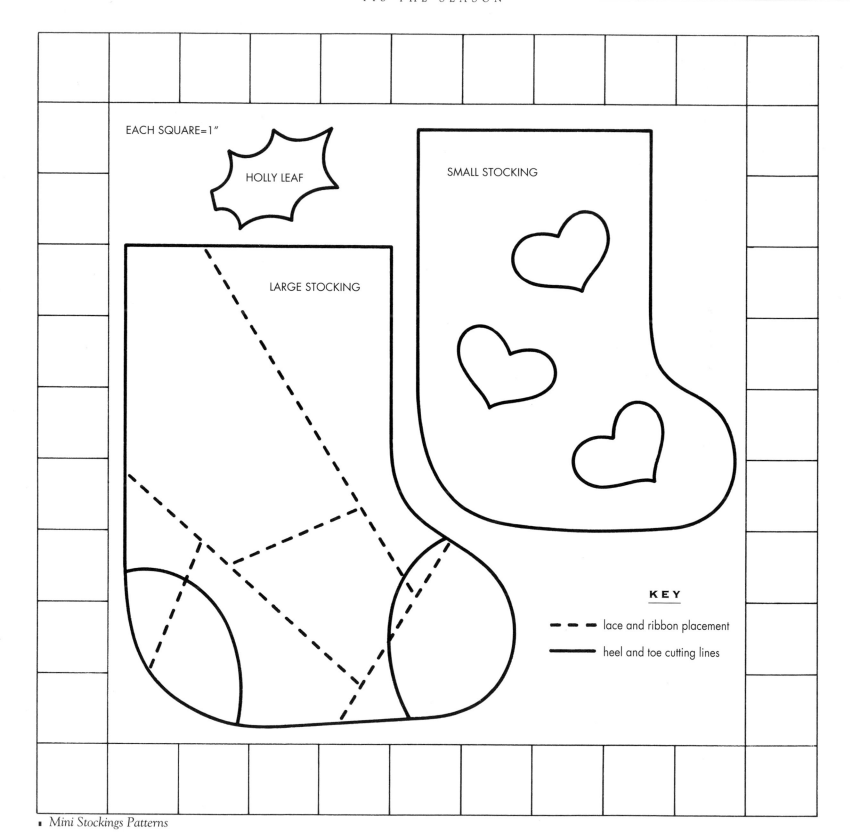

EACH SQUARE=1"

HOLLY LEAF

SMALL STOCKING

LARGE STOCKING

KEY

- - - - lace and ribbon placement

——— heel and toe cutting lines

■ *Mini Stockings Patterns*

around holly. Let dry completely. Glue jewels in place for berries. Fold 6" piece of ribbon in half and glue at top corner for hanging loop.

HEART STOCKING: Enlarge pattern on page 36 (see page 25, "Enlarging Patterns") for small stocking and trace onto red felt. Cut out for front. Trace and cut out three small hearts from white, using pinking shears. Trace stocking pattern onto white felt, adding ¼" to all sides. Cut out using pinking shears for back. Measure and cut one piece, 1½" x 9½", from white for cuff. Trace around cuff onto red felt, adding ¼" on all sides. Cut out using pinking shears. Position hearts on stocking front and, using six strands of embroidery floss, sew on with running stitches. Center red front, hearts facing up, on white back. Topstitch, leaving top edge open. Center white cuff piece on red cuff piece. Using red embroidery floss, sew together with running stitches. With wrong side of cuff against right side of stocking, glue cuff to top edge of stocking, wrapping around stocking and overlapping at center of back. Fold 6" piece of narrow ribbon in half and glue at top corner for hanging loop. Tie bow with wide ribbon and glue at hanging loop. Trim ends of ribbon.

HOLLY STOCKING: Enlarge pattern on page 36 (see page 25, "Enlarging Patterns") for large stocking and trace one onto green felt. Cut out for front. Trace pattern onto red felt, adding ¼" to all sides. Cut out using pinking shears for back. Trace and cut out one heel and toe piece from red. Measure and cut one piece, 1½" x 9½", from white for cuff. Trace around cuff onto red felt, adding ¼" to all sides. Cut out using pinking shears. Trace and cut out two holly motifs from green, reversing one. Center green front on red back. Topstitch, leaving top edge open. Glue heel and toe in position. Using green glitter paint, draw stitch lines around stocking, heel, and toe. Let dry completely. Center white cuff piece on red cuff and glue together. With wrong side of cuff against right side of stocking, glue cuff to top edge of stocking, wrapping around stocking and overlapping at center of back. Following photograph, glue holly pieces to center of cuff. Using green glitter paint, draw stitch lines

GLITTER STOCKING: Enlarge pattern on page 36 (see page 25, "Enlarging Patterns") for small stocking and trace two onto green felt. Cut out. Place together, aligning edges, and topstitch, leaving top edge open. Measure and cut one piece, 1½" x 9½", from white for cuff. Trace around cuff onto red felt, adding ¼" to all sides. Cut out using pinking shears. Center white cuff piece on red cuff, and glue together. With wrong side of cuff against right side of stocking, glue cuff to top edge of stocking, wrapping around stocking and overlapping at center of back. Using thin coat of clear glitter paint and paintbrush, paint cuff. Let dry completely. Using green glitter paint, draw stitch lines along machine stitching of cuff and stocking. Using green glitter paint, write name on cuff. Following photograph, glue stars and jewels in place as desired. Fold 6" piece of narrow ribbon in half and glue at top corner for hanging loop.

Elegant Holiday Place Mats

Create a tasteful ambiance for your holiday dinner parties. Each of these stenciled place mat sets has a distinctive look that is quick and easy to attain.

Delicate golden ribbons adorn dressy moiré fabric mats to create a perfect backdrop for a holiday table setting. A quilt block motif in rich Christmas colors will look perfect in either a country or a traditional setting. The Leaf-Stenciled Place Mat offers a sophisticated look that reminds one of the dappled sunlight of autumn.

GOLDEN RIBBONS PLACE MAT AND NAPKIN

SIZES

- Place mats are 12" x 18". Napkins are 17" square.

YOU WILL NEED

FOR TWO PLACE SETTINGS:
- 1½ yd white moiré fabric, 45" wide
- ½ yd paper-backed fusible interfacing
- 2 oz squeeze bottle fabric paint in gold
- Stencil paper and stencil brushes, ½"
- Water-soluble fabric marker and fine permanent marker
- Metal ruler, craft knife, and pencil
- Masking tape and rubber cement
- Matching thread and pins
- Newspapers and plastic wrap

DIRECTIONS

NOTE: Cover work surface with newspapers and plastic wrap. Let paints dry completely between steps. Following manufacturer's instructions, heat-set paint. Directions are for one place mat and napkin.

STENCILING: For place mat, draw two rectangles, 12" x 18", on white fabric using water-soluble marker. Cut out, adding ½" around all sides for seam allowance. Cut out an 18" square for each napkin. Place one rectangle on work surface and pin to secure. Using water-soluble marker, measure and mark a 1½" border along all sides. Lay masking tape along each line towards center of place mat to create a straight, sharp paint line. Cut tape at border line in corners. Using stencil brush and working out from tape to edge, paint borders gold. When painting near masking tape, "stomp" brush in an up-and-down motion to achieve a crisp and clean edge. Remove masking tape and let paint dry completely. Prepare and paint borders of napkin in same manner as place mat. Trace bow motif pattern onto stencil paper with permanent marker. Using craft knife, cut out stencil, making clean cuts. Coat

back of stencil with rubber cement and let dry. Following photograph, place bow stencil in center of one side of napkin, 1¼" in from border. Using stencil brush, paint stencil gold.

PLACE MAT ASSEMBLY: Cut a piece of fusible interfacing, 12" x 18". Following manufacturer's instructions, fuse interfacing to wrong side of place mat back. With right sides together, sew around front and back, using ½" seam allowance and leaving a 3" opening for turning. Trim seams, clip corners, and turn. Whipstitch opening closed.

NAPKIN ASSEMBLY: Serge or zigzag stitch around all four sides of napkin. Turn edges ½" to wrong side, tucking at corners. Topstitch around all four sides.

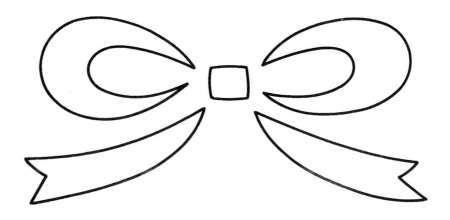

- Bow Motif Pattern (actual size)

SEASON'S GREETINGS
MEILLEURS VOEUX
С НОВЫМ ГОДОМ

FELICES
FIESTAS

St. Nicholas

QUILT BLOCK MOTIF PLACE MAT AND NAPKIN

SIZES

■ Place mats are 12" x 18". Napkins are 16" square.

YOU WILL NEED

FOR TWO PLACE SETTINGS:

■ $1/2$ yd natural quilted muslin, 45" wide
■ 1 yd natural muslin, 45" wide
■ $1/2$ yd paper-backed fusible interfacing
■ 2 oz squeeze bottles fabric paint in red and green
■ 1 pkg green bias tape
■ 2 pkgs green extra-wide bias tape
■ Stencil paper and stencil brushes, $1/2$"
■ Water-soluble fabric marker and fine permanent marker
■ Metal ruler, craft knife, paper punch, and pencil
■ Masking tape and rubber cement
■ Matching thread and pins
■ Newspapers and plastic wrap

DIRECTIONS

NOTES: Cover work surface with newspapers and plastic wrap. Let paints dry completely between steps. Following manufacturer's instructions, heat-set paint. Directions are for one place mat and napkin.

STENCILING: Using water-soluble marker, draw one rectangle, 12" x 18", on quilted muslin for place mat front. Draw a second rectangle, same size, on muslin for back. Cut out both pieces. Cut out a 16" square from muslin for napkin. Trace quilt motif pattern onto stencil paper with permanent marker. Using craft knife, cut out stencil, making clean cuts.

Use paper punch for circular holes. Coat back of stencil with rubber cement and let dry completely. Place front on work surface and pin to secure. Following photograph, arrange and mark stencil placement with water-soluble marker. Position middle circle center 3" in from one short edge. Overlap side and center circles by one leaf motif. Using stencil brush, paint red areas of motif. "Stomp" brush in an up-and-down motion to achieve a crisp and clean edge. Wipe stencil clean before changing colors. When red areas are completely dry, replace stencils and paint green areas. Mark $1½$" in from edges of one corner of napkin, for

placement guide. Place stencil in corner with one leaf motif facing into corner. Using stencil brush, paint stencil red and green as above.

PLACE MAT ASSEMBLY: Cut a piece of fusible interfacing, 12" x 18". Following manufacturer's instructions, fuse interfacing to wrong side of place mat back. With wrong sides together, topstitch front and back together, using $1/4$" seam allowance. Bind edges with extra-wide bias tape, overlapping corners and ends.

NAPKIN ASSEMBLY: Bind edges with bias tape, overlapping corners and ends.

■ *Quilt Motif Pattern (actual size)*

LEAF-STENCILED PLACE MAT AND NAPKIN

SIZES

- Place mats are 12" x 18". Napkins are 16" square.

YOU WILL NEED

FOR TWO PLACE SETTINGS:

- 1 yd white linen fabric, 60" wide
- ½ yd paper-backed fusible interfacing
- 2 oz squeeze bottles acrylic paint in yellow oxide, raw sienna, burnt sienna, burnt umber, green, magenta, metallic gold, dark green, and dark red
- Small natural sponge
- Stencil paper and stencil brushes, ½"
- Water-soluble fabric marker and fine permanent marker
- Metal ruler, craft knife, and paint pan
- Rubber cement
- Hot-glue gun and glue sticks
- Matching thread and pins
- Newspapers and plastic wrap

DIRECTIONS

NOTES: Cover work surface with newspapers and plastic wrap. Let paints dry completely between steps. Following manufacturer's instructions, heat-set paint. Directions are for one place mat and napkin.

STENCILING: Using water-soluble marker, draw two rectangles, 12" x 18", on white fabric for place mat front and back. Cut out, adding ½" around all sides for seam allowance. Cut out an 18" square for napkin. Trace leaf motif pattern onto stencil paper with permanent marker. Using craft knife, cut out stencil making clean cuts. Coat back of stencil with rubber cement and let dry completely. Place one rectangle of fabric for front on work surface and pin to secure. Squeeze some of each color paint onto paint pan. Add burnt umber to green and magenta and mix for desired shade. Following photograph, arrange leaves stencil on rectangle. Stencil, using colors as desired. "Stomp" brush in an up-and-down motion to achieve a crisp and clean edge. Wipe stencil clean when paint has built up on it and before changing color. Dip sponge in metallic gold and dab lightly over each leaf. Dab lightly between leaves with metallic gold. Thin burnt sienna with small amount of water and dip stencil brush into paint. Splatter paint lightly across fabric.

PLACE MAT ASSEMBLY: Cut a piece of fusible interfacing, 12" x 18". Following manufacturer's instructions, fuse interfacing to wrong side of place mat back. With right sides together, sew front and back, using ½" seam allowance and leaving a 3" opening for turning. Trim seams, clip corners, and turn. Whipstitch opening closed.

NAPKIN ASSEMBLY: Serge or zigzag stitch around all four sides of napkins. Turn edges 1" to wrong side, tucking at corners. Topstitch around all four sides.

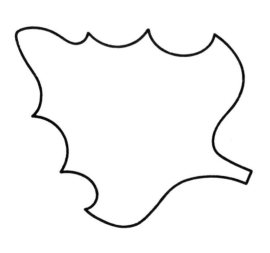

- *Leaf Motif Pattern (actual size)*

KITCHEN SWAG AND WREATH

During the holidays, more than ever, the kitchen is at the heart of the home. So don't forget to include the kitchen this year when decorating the house for Christmas. This lush swag and wreath will lend a festive feeling. Plump garlic bulbs, colorful chili peppers, and fragrant bay leaves together are remarkably Christmasy.

SIZES

- Swag is 65" long. Wreath is 8" diameter.

YOU WILL NEED

FOR BOTH PROJECTS:
- 1 pkg red florist's sinamay ribbon, 1½" wide
- Florist's wire
- Hot-glue gun and glue sticks
- Small wire cutters and craft scissors

FOR KITCHEN SWAG:
- 2 bunches dried eucalyptus
- 1 bunch dried baby's breath
- 6 dried wheat stalks
- 2 small heads garlic
- 24 dried red chili peppers
- 36 large whole bay leaves
- Stem wire and florist's tape

FOR KITCHEN WREATH:
- 8" foam wreath
- ¼ pound red lentils
- ¼ pound whole bay leaves
- 8 dried red chili peppers
- 1 head garlic
- Craft glue and paintbrush

DIRECTIONS

KITCHEN SWAG: Twist florist's wire together, forming a 60" long strip with hanging loops at each end. Cover wire, but not loops, with florist's tape. Spread out and position eucalyptus along florist's wire, cutting and saving small pretty ends for filling in. Secure eucalyptus to florist's wire with wire. Make three ribbon loops, each 8" long. Cut two pieces of ribbon, 12" and 14", for streamers. Trim ends of streamers. Following photograph, overlap loops and streamers to form a bow, and secure at center with wire. Cover center wire with ribbon and glue in place at back. Make a second bow in same manner. Make three chili nosegays by gluing six bay leaves together in the shape of a "V," approximately 5" wide, overlapping leaves. Attach stems of eight chilis together with wire. Glue peppers to bay leaves. Make three garlic nosegays by gluing bay leaves in same manner as for chili nosegays. Cut head of garlic in half and glue to center of bay leaves. Following photograph, position chili and garlic nosegays as desired. Slide several sprigs of baby's breath under each nosegay and secure with wire. Position bows as desired and secure with wire. Arrange baby's breath and three wheat stalks to overhang loops of swag. Secure with wire. Fill in bare spots of swag with leftover foliage.

KITCHEN WREATH: Brush one side of wreath with craft glue. Sprinkle with lentils, covering completely. Let dry completely. Turn wreath over and cover opposite side in same manner. Bend florist's wire in half and twist into a hanging loop. Wrap around wreath and secure. Glue bay leaves around wreath, overlapping edges and allowing lentils to show through. Save best-looking leaves for wreath's front. Arrange chili peppers in a small pile and glue together. Following photograph, position and glue in place. Cut head of garlic in half and glue both halves in place. Make two ribbon loops, each 7" long. Cut a piece of ribbon, 10" long, for streamer. Trim ends of ribbon. Following photograph, overlap loops and streamer to form a bow, and secure at center with wire. Cover center wire with ribbon and glue in place at back of bow. Glue in place on wreath as desired.

The Spirit of Giving

DON'T THINK OF LAST-MINUTE AS
LESS IMPORTANT! THE LUCKY
RECIPIENTS OF ANY OF THESE
GIFTS WILL BE THRILLED WITH
YOUR THOUGHTFULNESS. WHO
WOULDN'T ADORE ONE OF THESE
FAMILY HOLIDAY SWEATSHIRTS?
AND THESE BEAUTIFUL GIFT
WRAPPINGS MAKE EACH GIFT
UNIQUE FROM THE OUTSIDE IN.

STAMP ART

Put your personal stamp on some of the gifts you give this Christmas. Ready-made stamps come in an endless array of sizes and designs, and ink pads come in a rainbow of colors. Many shops offer custom-made stamps if you have a special request. Any unpainted wood item can be instantly transformed into a whimsical, funky, or pretty gift with quick but careful application of "stamp art." Before painting the piece, be sure it is sanded smooth and wiped clean with a tack cloth.

SIZES

- Tray is 12" x 17". Domed Box is 5" x 7¼" x 2½" high. Nesting Boxes are 4½", 6", and 7" diameter. Birdhouse is 4" x 9". Tissue Box is 5" x 5" x 5¾" high.

YOU WILL NEED

FOR ALL PROJECTS:
- Paintbrushes
- Clear spray sealer
- Newspapers and plastic wrap

FOR TRAY:
- Unfinished wooden tray
- 2 oz squeeze bottle acrylic paint in light turquoise
- Tulip, fern, and small flower rubber stamps
- Green, red, and blue ink stamp pads

FOR DOMED BOX:
- Unfinished wooden domed box
- 2 oz squeeze bottle acrylic paint in light blue
- Basket weave and star rubber stamps
- Orange ink stamp pad

FOR NESTING BOXES:
- 3 unfinished wooden round nesting band boxes
- 2 oz squeeze bottles acrylic paint in peach and light blue
- Basket weave and large chrysanthemum rubber stamps
- Royal blue and red ink stamp pads

FOR BIRDHOUSE:
- Unfinished wooden birdhouse
- 2 oz squeeze bottles acrylic paint in yellow, light blue, and light turquoise
- Tulip, small butterfly, large butterfly, sun, and small flower rubber stamps
- Purple, turquoise, and red ink stamp pads

FOR TISSUE BOX:
- Unfinished wooden tissue box
- 2 oz squeeze bottle acrylic paint in cream
- Fern and small flower rubber stamps
- Royal blue and turquoise ink stamp pads

DIRECTIONS

NOTE: Cover work surface with newspapers and plastic wrap. Let paints dry completely between steps.

TRAY: Paint entire tray with two coats of light turquoise. Following photograph and using green stamp pad, stamp fern motifs around outer edges of floor of tray and along inner sides. Using red stamp pad, stamp tulip motifs inside fern motifs and in center of tray. Using blue stamp pad, stamp small flower motifs in center. Spray with two coats of sealer.

DOMED BOX: Paint entire box and lid with two coats of light blue. Following photograph and using orange stamp pad, stamp star motifs around sides of box and top of lid. Stamp basket weave around sides of box lid. Spray with two coats of sealer.

NESTING BOXES: Paint all three boxes and lids with two coats of paint. Use peach for two smaller boxes and light blue for larger box. Following photograph and using royal blue stamp pad for smallest and largest box and red stamp pad for medium box, stamp chrysanthemum motifs around sides of box and top of lid. Stamp basket weave around sides of box lid. Spray with two coats of sealer.

BIRDHOUSE: Paint entire birdhouse and lid with two coats of yellow. Paint perches with light blue and light turquoise. Following photograph and using turquoise stamp pad, stamp sun in top center of each side. Using red stamp pad, stamp tulips on each side at bottom of birdhouse. Using turquoise and purple stamp pads, randomly stamp small and large butterflies around box. Using turquoise stamp pad, cover roof with small flower motifs. Spray with two coats of sealer.

TISSUE BOX: Paint entire box with two coats of cream. Following photograph and using turquoise stamp pad, stamp fern motifs along top edge and top of box. Using royal blue stamp pad, stamp small flower motifs randomly around sides and between ferns on top. Spray with two coats of sealer.

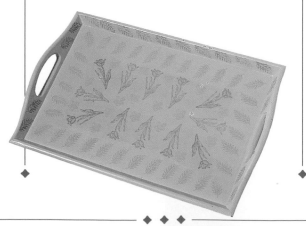

GIFTS FOR GARDENERS

Most gardeners find it very difficult to forget about gardening when the summer season ends. Looking through picture books, reading gardening magazines, and anticipating the arrival of the seed catalogs helps extend the season.

These thoughtful Gifts for Gardeners are both practical and attractive and will bring some cheery signs of spring into the hearts of your green-thumbed friends.

SIZES

- Watering Can is 10" high. Garden Tools, as desired. Garden Gloves, as desired. Flowerpots are 5" and 7" diameter.

YOU WILL NEED

FOR ALL PROJECTS:
- Acrylic gel medium
- Sharp-pointed scissors and pencil
- Foam paintbrushes, ½" and 1"
- 1 can clear spray sealer, glossy

FOR WATERING CAN:
- Plastic watering can
- 1 sheet allover flower-patterned gift wrap

FOR GARDEN TOOLS:
- Trowel, shovel, and spade with smooth handles
- Assorted pictures of flowers clipped from seed catalogs or gift wrap
- Medium-fine sandpaper and paper towels for wooden handles

FOR GARDEN GLOVES:
- 1 pair of garden gloves
- 2 oz squeeze bottles acrylic paint in red, green, and blue
- Small long-bristle paintbrush

FOR PAINTED FLOWERPOT:
- 7" clay flowerpot
- 2 oz squeeze bottles acrylic paint in yellow and blue

FOR SUNFLOWER FLOWERPOT:
- 5" clay flowerpot
- Natural sponge
- Small long-bristle paintbrush
- 2 oz squeeze bottles acrylic paint in yellow, green, blue, and rust

FOR PRIMROSE FLOWERPOT:
- 5" clay flowerpot
- Small long-bristle paintbrush
- 2 oz squeeze bottles acrylic paint in yellow, blue, green, and red

DIRECTIONS

WATERING CAN: Using watering can as pattern, lay it down on gift wrap and trace large areas to be covered. Cut out. Following manufacturer's instructions, cover back of gift wrap with gel medium and wrap around can, smoothing out air bubbles with fingers as you work. Be sure to cover entire back of gift wrap with gel medium and smooth edges to secure. Clip paper as needed to smooth around corners and curves. When large areas are covered, cut smaller pieces of wrapping paper and fill in uncovered areas, overlapping paper as needed. Wrap strips of paper around spout and handle, covering entire areas. Let dry completely. Spray with two coats of sealer.

GARDEN TOOLS: If using wooden-handled tools, sand off finish. Wipe clean with paper towels. Arrange pictures of flowers clipped from a seed catalog or wrap, as desired. Choose similar colors or flowers for each tool handle. Cut pictures into strips and, following manufacturer's instructions, cover back with gel medium. Wrap around handles, smoothing out air bubbles with fingers as you work. Be sure to cover entire back of strips with gel medium and smooth edges to secure. Clip strips as needed to smooth around corners and curves. Overlap paper as needed. Let dry completely. Spray with two coats of sealer.

GARDEN GLOVES: Using primrose pattern on page 52, trace onto wrist of each glove. Following photograph and using small paintbrush, paint design. Let dry completely.

PAINTED FLOWERPOT: Using 1" foam brush, paint entire pot with two coats of yellow. Let dry completely. Using 1" foam brush, paint a blue stripe in center of rim. Using ½" foam brush, make one blue squiggle line ½" below rim on base of pot and one ½" above bottom of pot. Using 1" foam brush, paint a second stripe centered on base of pot. Let dry completely. Spray with two coats of sealer.

SUNFLOWER FLOWERPOT: Using 1" foam brush, paint rim with one coat of yellow. Using sponge, dab rust over yellow. Using 1" foam brush, paint entire base green. Using sponge, dab blue over green. Using sunflower pattern on page 52, trace onto base of pot while paints are still slightly wet. Paint petals yellow with sides of 1" foam brush. Dip sponge in yellow paint, then rust paint, and in a circular motion, dab center of sunflower. With small paintbrush, add small rust dots to center of sunflower. Outline yellow petals with green.

Let dry completely. Spray with two coats of sealer.

PRIMROSE FLOWERPOT: Using 1" foam brush, paint pot yellow. Let dry completely. Using primrose pattern below, trace and center along entire rim. Following photograph and using small paintbrush, paint primrose pattern. Outline leaf shape and draw in leaf veins with red. Let dry completely. Spray with two coats of sealer.

• *Sunflower Flowerpot Pattern (actual size)*

• *Primrose Pattern for Garden Gloves (actual size)*

COLOR KEY

R red

B blue

Y yellow

G green

• *Primrose Flowerpot Pattern (actual size)*

Scented Sachets

Fragrant sachets make much-appreciated gifts. These are quick to make and everyone seems to love their refreshing scents. Either the clean crisp Pine Sachets or the more feminine Black and Gold Lace Sachets would make perfect gifts for casual friends, co-workers, or teachers. Or use them as stocking stuffers or as scented tags on gift boxes.

PINE SACHETS

SIZE

• Sachets are approximately 4".

YOU WILL NEED

FOR ALL SACHETS:
• Pine or balsam needles collected from trees or purchased from craft shop
• Essential pine oil from health-food store
• Matching thread
• Scissors, ruler, and pencil

FOR EMBROIDERED SACHET:
• 10" square dark ecru linen
• 6" square cotton print fabric for backing
• 1 skein each embroidery floss in green and brown
• Embroidery hoop and needle
• Dressmaker's carbon
• 1 pkg red rickrack

FOR APPLIQUÉD TREE SACHET:
• 6" x 12" rectangle cream print cotton
• Assorted scraps of yellow, green, and brown fabrics
• 6" square paper-backed fusible web

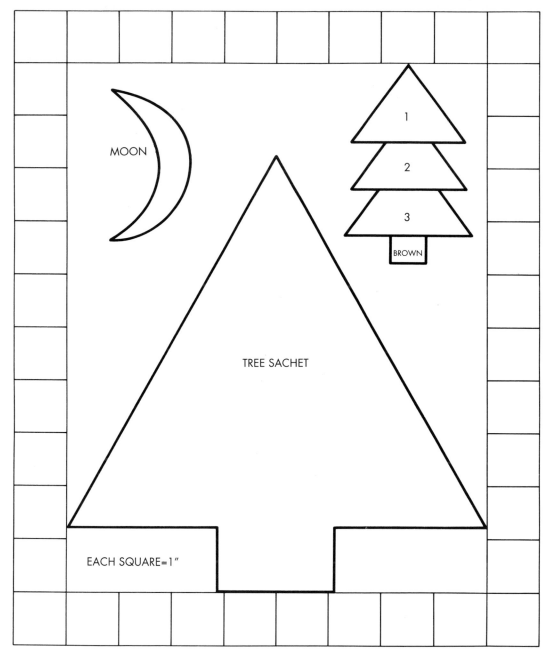

MOON

1

2

3

BROWN

TREE SACHET

EACH SQUARE=1"

- *Pine Sachet Patterns*

- **Black line permanent marker**
- **1 pkg red loop braid edging**

FOR TREE-SHAPED SACHET:
- **8" square each of 2 green print cotton fabrics**
- **1 pkg gold metallic rickrack**
- **10 assorted small glittery buttons**
- **Craft glue**

DIRECTIONS

NOTE: Sprinkle pine or balsam with several drops of pine oil to enhance scent. Mix and let stand for 1 hour.

EMBROIDERED SACHET: Using pattern on page 55, trace pine branch motif onto center of right side of linen using dressmaker's carbon. Insert linen in embroidery hoop and using three strands of floss and outline stitch, embroider design. Using three strands of brown embroidery floss and wrapping floss around needle four times, work French knots as indicated on page 55. Remove from hoop and press linen on wrong side. Draw a 6" square with embroidery in center and cut out. Baste rickrack around linen square just inside the outer edge. With right sides together, using a ¼" seam allowance, and catching rickrack, sew linen and backing fabric together, leaving a small opening for turning. Turn sachet right side out. Fill with pine or balsam needles. Whipstitch opening closed.

APPLIQUÉD TREE SACHET: Enlarge pattern at left (see page 25, "Enlarging Patterns") and trace 3 tree sections, tree trunk, and moon onto paper backing of fusible web. Following manufacturer's instructions and photograph, fuse web to wrong sides of assorted cotton scraps. Cut out pieces. Cut cream fabric into two 6" squares. Following photograph, fuse

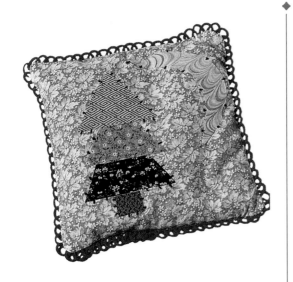

pieces to right side of one cream square as desired. With marker, draw small lines to resemble overcast stitches around each fused piece. Baste loop edging just inside the outer edge of square on the right side, with loops toward center. With right sides together, using a ¼" seam allowance, and catching loop edging, sew two pieces of cream fabric together, leaving a small opening for turning. Turn sachet right side out. Fill with pine or balsam needles. Whipstitch opening closed.

TREE-SHAPED SACHET: Enlarge pattern on page 54 (see page 25, "Enlarging Patterns") and trace tree shape onto wrong side of both squares of green fabric. Cut out. Baste rickrack just inside the outer edge on right side of one tree shape. Cut an 8½" length of rickrack and, following photograph, sew or glue diagonally across tree. With right sides together, using a ¼" seam allowance, and catching rickrack, sew green fabric pieces together, leaving a small opening for turning. Turn sachet right side out. Sew or glue buttons randomly along rickrack length. Fill with pine or balsam needles. Whipstitch opening closed.

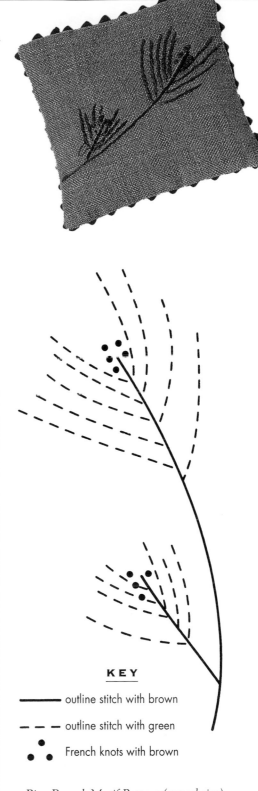

FRENCH KNOTS

STEP 1: Bring needle up through fabric where knot is to be made (1). Wind thread around point of needle two or three times.

STEP 2: Insert needle into fabric close to spot where needle emerged (2). Pull to wrong side, holding stitch in place.

KEY

——— outline stitch with brown

– – – outline stitch with green

•••• French knots with brown

▪ *Pine Branch Motif Pattern (actual size)*

BLACK AND GOLD LACE SACHETS

SIZES

- Sachets are approximately 3" to 4".

YOU WILL NEED

FOR EACH SACHET:

- ½ yd black and gold lace fabric with scalloped edge, 45" wide
- Matching thread
- 1 yd sheer red ribbon, ½" wide
- ¼ yd green ribbon, 1" wide
- 3 assorted cherub charms
- 1 small bag potpourri
- Scissors, ruler, and pencil

DIRECTIONS

HEART AND SQUARE SACHETS: Enlarge pattern below (see page 25, "Enlarging Patterns") and trace sachet shapes onto lace fabric. Cut two each of chosen shape from fabric for each sachet. With wrong sides together, topstitch along stitch lines around all sides, leaving a small opening for filling. Fill sachet with potpourri. Topstitch opening closed. Tie a 3" bow, using a double strand of red ribbon. Tack bow to sachet. Sew cherub charm to center of bow.

BALL SACHET: Cut a 6¾" x 10½" strip of lace, with scalloped edge of lace along one long edge. With right side in, fold strip in half crosswise. Using a ¼" seam allowance, stitch across short ends to form a loop. Press. Sew a row of gathering stitches 1½" in from scalloped edge for top and another row ¼" in from opposite long edge for bottom. Pull up bottom gathers tightly and tie. Trim thread. Turn right side out. Fill tube with potpourri and pull up top gathers. Tie to secure. Tie a 3½" bow with green ribbon and tack onto sachet. Sew cherub charm to center of bow.

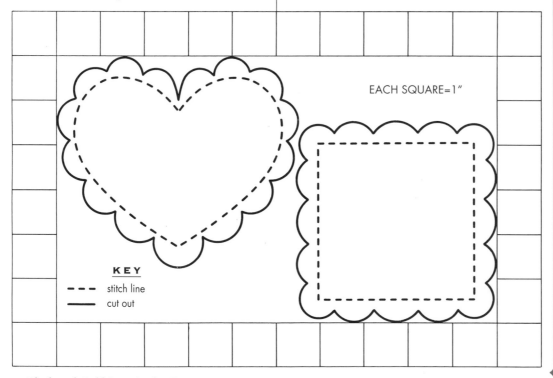

EACH SQUARE=1"

KEY

--- stitch line
— cut out

- *Black and Gold Lace Sachet Patterns*

Family Holiday Sweatshirts

Just about everyone has a favorite sweatshirt. Sweatshirts are versatile, comfortable, easy to wash, and available in great colors. Wouldn't it be fun to make holiday sweatshirts for every member of your family? Fused-on fabrics, easy sewing techniques, and fabric paints make it simple to create a group of fabulous Family Holiday Sweatshirts.

CELESTIAL SWEATSHIRT

SIZE

- As desired.

YOU WILL NEED

- Sweatshirt
- 2 oz squeeze bottle acrylic paint in gold
- Stencil paper and stencil brushes, ½"
- Craft knife, permanent marker, and paint pan
- Rubber cement, newspapers, and plastic wrap

DIRECTIONS

NOTES: Cover work surface with newspapers and plastic wrap. Let paints dry completely between steps. Following manufacturer's instructions, heat-set paint.

STENCILING: Enlarge pattern at right (see page 25, "Enlarging Patterns") and trace onto stencil paper with permanent marker. Using craft knife, cut out stencil, making clean cuts. Coat back of stencil with rubber cement and

EACH SQUARE=1"

- *Christmas Tree Sweatshirt (far left); Celestial Sweatshirt Stencil Pattern (above); Celestial Sweatshirt (left and right)*

let dry completely. Place sweatshirt on work surface and pin to secure. Following photograph, arrange and paint sun motif onto front of sweatshirt. "Stomp" brush in an up-and-down motion to achieve a crisp and clean edge. Wipe stencil clean when paint has built up. Randomly arrange and paint five stars around sun.

APPLIQUÉD SWEATSHIRTS

SIZES

- As desired.

YOU WILL NEED

FOR CHRISTMAS TREE SWEATSHIRT:
- Sweatshirt
- ¼ yd paper-backed fusible web
- Small amounts 8 green print cotton fabrics for tree
- Small amount brown print cotton fabric for tree trunk
- Small amounts plaid cotton fabric for stars
- 1 pkg gold metallic rickrack
- 2 oz squeeze bottle glitter fabric paint in gold
- 12 assorted glittery buttons
- Scissors and pencil

FOR ANGEL SWEATSHIRT:
- Sweatshirt
- Small amount paper-backed fusible web
- Small amounts 4 pink print cotton fabrics for angel dresses
- Small amounts 4 dark gold print cotton fabrics for angel wings and stars
- Small amounts 4 cream print cotton fabrics for angel heads and feet

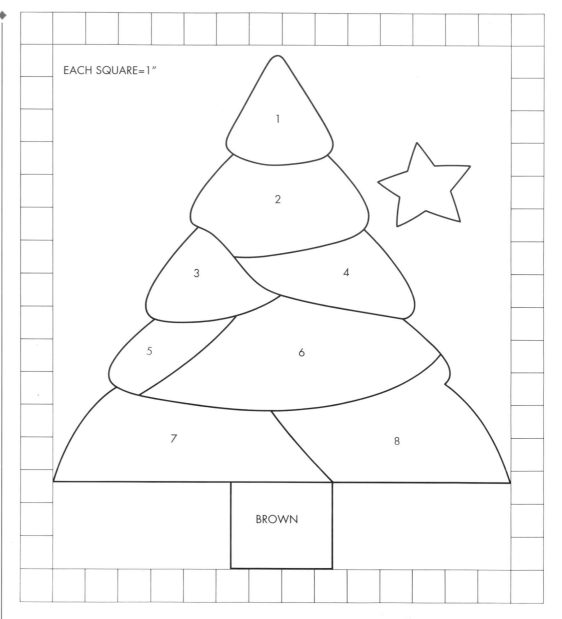

EACH SQUARE=1"

BROWN

- *Christmas Tree Sweatshirt Pattern (above); Christmas Tree Sweatshirt (right)*

- Small piece gold lamé fabric for stars
- 8 assorted small buttons
- 2 oz squeeze bottle glitter fabric paint in gold
- Scissors and pencil

FOR MITTEN SWEATSHIRT:
- Sweatshirt
- Small amount paper-backed fusible web
- 8" square each red and green print cotton fabric
- 8" x 16" rectangle backing fabric
- 1 pkg red jumbo rickrack
- 1 spool each metallic gold and white thread
- Scissors and pencil

- *Angel Sweatshirt (above); Angel and Mitten Sweatshirt Patterns (below)*

DIRECTIONS

CHRISTMAS TREE SWEATSHIRT: Enlarge pattern on page 60 (see page 25, "Enlarging Patterns") and trace six stars, one each of eight tree sections, and tree trunk onto paper backing of fusible web. Following manufacturer's instructions, fuse web onto wrong side of fabrics. Cut out pieces. Following photograph, arrange tree sections and stars onto front of sweatshirt as desired. Fuse pieces into place. Cut lengths of rickrack to outline sections of tree. Sew rickrack in place by hand or secure with a small amount of fabric paint. In same manner, randomly attach buttons to tree. Using gold glitter fabric paint, outline stars and tree, covering raw fabric edges. Let dry completely.

ANGEL SWEATSHIRT: Enlarge pattern at right (see page 25, "Enlarging Patterns") and trace four each of angel dresses, heads, pairs of feet, wings, and seven stars onto paper backing of fusible web. Following manufacturer's instructions, fuse web onto wrong side of fabrics. Cut out pieces. Fuse angel wings across lower

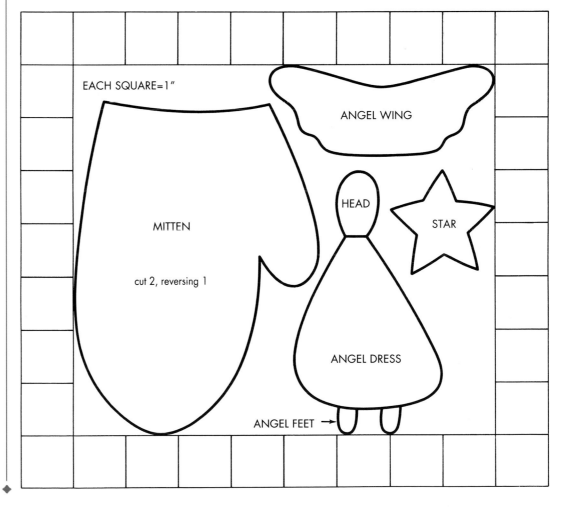

EACH SQUARE=1"

MITTEN

cut 2, reversing 1

ANGEL WING

HEAD

STAR

ANGEL DRESS

ANGEL FEET →

section of shirt. Fuse dresses over wings, then fuse heads and feet in place. Fuse four lamé stars beneath angel's feet and three stars, overlapped, on right shoulder of sweatshirt. Sew two buttons to front center of each angel or secure with a small amount of fabric paint. Using gold glitter fabric paint, paint halos over each angel's head.

MITTEN SWEATSHIRT: Enlarge pattern on page 61 (see page 25, "Enlarging Patterns") and trace two mittens onto paper backing of fusible web, reversing one. Following manufacturer's instructions, fuse web onto wrong side of red and green fabrics. Cut along marked line, then fuse mittens to wrong side of backing fabric. Cut mittens from backing fabric. Following photograph, pin mittens to front of sweatshirt. With gold thread in machine needle and white thread in bobbin, satin stitch mittens to sweatshirt, leaving upper edges unstitched so mittens can be used as pockets. Following photograph, position rickrack across opening of one mitten, then curve slightly toward neck. Bring around back of neck, then down to other mitten and across the top of opening. Sew rickrack in place by hand.

■ *Mitten Sweatshirt*

Wrapped in Style

Be sure to set aside some time during the last minute rush for wrapping presents. The simplest gifts have a lot more appeal when they are wrapped creatively. Many seemingly mundane household items can be recycled into clever gift presentations. Brown paper bags offer endless possibilities. Berry boxes make clever containers. And boxes of all sizes and shapes that you've hesitated to throw away will come in handy.

The ideas here are just for inspiration—you're certain to come up with more uses for the treasures in your scrap collection.

GIFT WRAPPINGS

SIZES
■ **Strawberry Baskets are 5½" square. Accordion Envelope is 6" wide. Round Box is 8" diameter. Grass Cloth Cookie Tin is 7" long.**

YOU WILL NEED
FOR STRAWBERRY BASKETS:
- 5½" strawberry baskets
- Acrylic gel medium and paintbrush
- 2 oz squeeze bottles acrylic paint in yellow and green
- Assorted empty seed packages
- Scissors
- Clear spray sealer

■ *Strawberry Basket Wraps (left); Accordion Envelope (right)*

■ *Round Box (left); Grass Cloth Cookie Tin (right)*

FOR ACCORDION ENVELOPE:
- 6" accordion envelope
- Small-patterned and solid-colored origami paper
- 2 oz squeeze bottle acrylic paint in red
- Acrylic gel medium and paintbrush
- 12" length green grosgrain ribbon, 1" wide
- Scissors
- Clear spray sealer

FOR ROUND BOX:
- 8" round box with lid
- Assorted maps
- Acrylic gel medium and paintbrush
- Scissors
- Clear spray sealer

FOR GRASS CLOTH COOKIE TIN:
- 7" cylindrical cookie tin
- 15" square grass cloth
- Strips of raffia
- Twig and painted leaf

DIRECTIONS

STRAWBERRY BASKETS: Paint strawberry baskets with green or yellow paint. Cut out pictures from front of seed packages as desired. Arrange on baskets, then remove and, following manufacturer's instructions, cover back of each with gel medium. Place in position, smoothing out air bubbles with fingers as you work. Be sure to cover entire back with gel medium and smooth edges to secure. Spray with two coats of sealer.

ACCORDION ENVELOPE: Paint accordion envelope red. Cut pieces of origami paper. Following photograph, arrange on envelope, then remove and, following manufacturer's instructions, cover back of each piece with gel medium. Place in position, smoothing out air bubbles with fingers as you work. Be sure to cover entire back with gel medium and smooth edges to secure. Tie envelope closed with length of ribbon. Trim ends of ribbon. Spray with two coats of sealer.

ROUND BOX: Using box and lids as patterns, lay them on maps and trace large areas to be covered. Mark box where you begin tracing so you know where to end. Add 1/2" to edge to be folded into lid and to top and bottom of box. Cut out. Following manufacturer's instructions, cover back of maps with gel medium and wrap around lid or box. Center map on box so 1/2" extends at top and at bottom. Position map on lid so 1/2" extends to bottom. Smooth out any air bubbles with fingers as you work. Be sure to cover entire back with gel medium and smooth edges to secure. Fold 1/2" over edges or onto bottom. Clip paper as needed to smooth around curves. When large areas are covered, cut smaller pieces of map to fill uncovered areas, folding over edge of box or lid or to bottom of box. Spray with two coats of sealer.

GRASS CLOTH COOKIE TIN: Wrap piece of grass cloth diagonally around cookie tin. Tie ends closed with strips of raffia. Tie twigs and painted leaf to ends of raffia.

EMERGENCY WRAPS

Start filing away wrapping paper and ribbons on the day after Christmas. Keep the prettiest papers, ribbons, and cards. The key to successful saving is to have a storage system, or at least one location where you put all the bits and pieces that you save during the year. Catalogs that specialize in tools to help people get organized often sell wrapping paper chests with compartments for ribbons, cards, and other decorations. If you put all your wrapping needs in one place, you will always be able to wrap in a hurry.

CHRISTMAS COOKING

PART

2

The
ideal holiday
party features fun,
sophisticated food that
seems to appear effortlessly,
while the hostess has time to mingle
with guests. Sound like a job for professional
caterers? The secret to successful entertaining
without hired help is meticulous planning and
make-ahead dishes that require only a light completing
touch at party or dinner time. In this section, you'll find
terrific party foods. Delicious appetizers include finger food
favorites and heartwarming soups. Crowd-pleasing entrées feature innovative
ideas as well as new approaches to the classics. Finishing touches offer special
occasions desserts and
a plethora of cookie
treats. But don't save
these recipes just for
the holidays; they taste
great all year round.

HOLIDAY MENUS

The holidays are here, and it's time to gather family and friends to share love, gifts, and good food. Get the season off to a festive start by choosing a date for an open house when friends can drop by to say Merry Christmas! You could offer spicy and colorful Tex-Mex fare or a tempting Tree-Trimming Dessert Buffet (see page 69).

Weekend brunch is another opportunity to get friends together for cozy chats and warming food and drink. A brunch menu of delicious, seasonal, make-ahead dishes is on page 69.

During this season, family meals also feature special dishes and table decorations that herald the arrival of Christmas. Your family's memories and traditions are made of these days and nights of candlelight, pine wreaths, and scrumptious food.

The following menus were developed from the three books in **Better Homes and Gardens®** *Countdown to Christmas* series. The stars indicate recipes from each book. If you don't have *Christmas On Its Way* or *Christmas 'Round the Corner*, use the alternative suggestions that are offered, or substitute your own favorite recipes.

> * **Christmas On Its Way**
> ** **Christmas 'Round the Corner**
> *** **'Tis the Season**

THANKSGIVING DAY DINNER

APPETIZERS
*** Watercress Soup
*** Mrs. D's Bacon Breadstix

ENTRÉE
*** Roast Turkey with Apple-Onion Stuffing
*** Pecan-Crusted Sweet Potatoes
** Stir-Fry Frozen Mixture or steamed mixed vegetables
Cranberry relish and * Sunshine Orange Slices
* Corn Sticks with butter and * Preserved Lemony Figs or cornbread with assorted jams

*** Orange-Red Onion Salad with Mixed Greens

DESSERT
** Pumpkin-Nut Roll or pumpkin pie

BEVERAGE
Dry white Riesling/milk/coffee

TEX-MEX BUFFET PARTY

APPETIZERS
*** Chili con Queso
Vegetable platter
*** Texas Caviar
Tortilla chips
*** Onion Bites

ENTRÉE
*** Feliz Navidad Taco Casserole
*** Oven-Baked Spanish Rice
* Corn Sticks with * Red and Green Bell
   Pepper Jelly or cornbread and butter
Relish tray: Pickled peppers
   * Pennsylvania Dutch Corn Relish
   Cubes of pepper cheese

DESSERT
** Mexican Chocolate Sugar Cookies or
   *** Chocolate Butter Cookies
Tangerines and grapes

BEVERAGE
Sangria/beer/soft drinks

TREE-TRIMMING DESSERT BUFFET

*** Cranberry-Berry Trifle
** Aunt Snookum's Chocolate Pound
   Cake or *** Triple Chocolate
   Cheesecake
** Buttery Spritz Cookies or shortbread
** Pecan Crescents or pecan cookies
** Fruit Granola Rolls or *** Stuffed
   Dried Fruit
*** Apple Dessert

BEVERAGE
Hot wassail punch/sparkling water/juices

HOLIDAY WEEKEND BRUNCH

ENTRÉE
*** Broccoli-Cheese Bake or ** Broccoli-
   Cheese Quiche
Crisp-cooked bacon strips
*** Orange-Red Onion Salad with Mixed
   Greens
** Whole-Wheat Dinner Rolls with
   * Strawberry Freezer Jam or purchased
   rolls and jam

DESSERT
*** Bananas Faster
** Mexican Chocolate Sugar Cookies or
   other cookies

BEVERAGE
Coffee/Bloody Marys/orange juice

COME FOR COCKTAILS

* Cheese Sticks or cheese-flavored breadsticks
*** Baked Chicken Nuggets with Honey Mustard or ** Chinese Pot Stickers with * Chinese Dipping Sauce
*** Spinach-Ham Fingers or *** Mrs. D's Bacon Breadstix
*** Yogurt Cheese-Pimiento Spread
Vegetable platter and crackers
Salted nuts
Christmas cookies

BEVERAGE
Cocktails/sparkling water/juices

CHRISTMAS IS FOR KIDS PARTY

*** Mrs. D's Bacon Breadstix
** Pete's-a Pizza or *** Baked Chicken Nuggets with Honey Mustard
*** Corn Stuffing Balls
Celery sticks stuffed with peanut butter
Cut-up fruit pieces

** Gingerbread People or other cookies

BEVERAGE
Juices/milk

CHRISTMAS EVE DINNER AT HOME

ENTRÉE
*** Shrimp Gruyère Crepes or ** Swedish Meatballs
Steamed green beans
*** Stuffed Tomatoes
** French Bread or purchased crusty bread with butter

DESSERT
*** Very Moist Gingerbread with Lemon Sauce or ** Patty's Shoe filled with ice cream and topped with * Toffee Sauce

BEVERAGE
Sauvignon Blanc or Pinot Chardonnay/ * Cranberry Cordial or other liqueur/ coffee/milk

CHRISTMAS DAY DINNER

APPETIZER
*** Christmas-in-California Soup

ENTRÉE
*** Rolled Rib Roast with Make-Ahead
    Popovers
*** Minnesota Wild Rice or * Herbed Rice
    Mix
*** Candied Carrots and Parsnips or
    steamed broccoli flowerets
*** Quick Mix Relishes

Mixed green salad with Chèvre cheese and
    toasted walnuts
* Basil Vinegar or red wine vinegar and
    olive oil dressing

DESSERT
*** Ricotta Christmas Tart or ** Cassata a
    la Little Italy

BEVERAGE
Gewürztraminer or California Merlot/
    coffee/milk

NEW YEAR'S EVE BUFFET

*** Cream Cheese Bar Tricks
*** Nathana's Baked Ham, thinly sliced
Mayonnaise and a variety of mustards,
    including * Homemade Mustard
Pumpernickel bread/** Whole-Wheat
    Dinner Rolls/** Cheddar Cheese and
    Onion Quick Bread
Potato salad
Relish tray: Cut fresh vegetables
    * Mom's Bread and Butter Pickles
    * Sunshine Orange Slices
    * Apple-Peach-Raisin Chutney

DESSERT
*** Deep Chocolate Applesauce Cake or
    ** Cinnamon-Chocolate Coffee Cake

BEVERAGE
Beer, champagne, or sparkling apple
    juice/sparkling water/soft drinks/coffee

CHRISTMAS BREAKFAST

ENTRÉE
Orange and grapefruit sections on spinach
    leaves sprinkled with pomegranate seeds
* Corn Waffles with * Brandied Jam Sauce
    or waffles with syrup
Sweet Italian sausages

BEVERAGE
* Hot Cocoa or hot chocolate/
    coffee/juices

CHAPTER 1

Holiday Hors d'Oeuvres and Starters

HORS D'OEUVRES AND STARTERS ARE MEANT TO SET THE MOOD OF A MEAL AND PREPARE THE PALATE FOR THE MAIN EVENT. THEY SHOULD ALSO KEEP GUESTS OCCUPIED WHILE THE HOSTESS MAKES LAST-MINUTE PREPARATIONS. MOST OF THESE

SENSATIONAL STARTERS CAN BE PREPARED A DAY OR SO BEFORE THE PARTY, SO YOU CAN CONCENTRATE ON GETTING EVERYTHING ELSE ON THE TABLE. AND THEY ALL TASTE GREAT—A SUGGESTION OF A GREAT MEAL TO FOLLOW.

MRS. D'S BACON BREADSTIX

These crispy treats are served as nibbles with drinks before dinner at parties given by Mrs. D.—a Park Avenue socialite. For make-ahead ease, refrigerate the baked breadsticks for up to 24 hours, then reheat them in a 350°F oven about 5 to 8 minutes until heated through, shortly before serving.

1 pound bacon
20 to 24, 6- to 8-inch thin, unflavored
   Italian breadsticks

Preheat the oven to 350°F. Cook half the bacon in a skillet over medium heat for about 5 minutes until partially cooked. Drain on paper towels. Repeat with the remaining bacon. Hold a breadstick in one hand and, beginning at one end of the breadstick, wrap a slice of partially cooked bacon around the breadstick in a spiral. (The breadsticks are fragile, so handle gently.) Place wrapped breadsticks on an ungreased baking sheet and bake for 10 to 15 minutes, or until crisp and brown. Drain on paper towels. Serve warm.

Makes 20 to 24.

▪ *Mrs. D's Bacon Breadstix*

SPINACH-HAM FINGERS

Spinach crepes wrapped around a minced ham filling and tied with chives, like little gifts, make ideal finger food for cocktail parties.

CREPES
1½ cups milk
1½ cups all-purpose flour
3 eggs
½ cup water
1 tablespoon cooking oil
½ teaspoon salt
¼ teaspoon ground nutmeg
1 package (10 ounces) frozen chopped spinach, thawed and well-drained
5 green onions, washed, trimmed, and chopped

FILLING
2 packages (3 ounces each) cream cheese, softened
2 cups finely chopped fully cooked lean ham
¼ cup mayonnaise or salad dressing
1½ teaspoons prepared mustard
2 tablespoons chopped pimientos
Long chives (optional)

TO MAKE THE CREPES: In a large bowl, combine the milk, flour, eggs, water, oil, salt, and nutmeg. Beat with a rotary beater until well-mixed. Stir in the spinach and onions.

Heat a lightly greased 6" skillet over medium heat. Remove from heat. Pour ¼ cup of the crepe batter into the skillet; lift and tilt the skillet, spreading batter to cover bottom of skillet. If necessary, spread the batter using a rubber spatula. Return to heat. Cook the crepe for 1 to 2 minutes or until browned on the bottom. Invert skillet over a paper towel-lined baking sheet and remove crepe. Repeat,

greasing the pan as needed, until all the batter is used, to make about 15 crepes. (Crepes can be stacked, separated by sheets of waxed paper, wrapped well in foil or plastic wrap, and refrigerated for up to 2 days or frozen for up to 1 month.)

TO MAKE THE FILLING: In a medium bowl, beat the cream cheese with an electric mixer until light and fluffy. Stir in the ham, mayonnaise or salad dressing, mustard, and pimientos; mix well. (Mixture can be covered and refrigerated for up to 2 days.)

TO MAKE THE ROLLS: Place a crepe on a flat surface, browned side down. Spread unbrowned side with about 2 tablespoons filling. Roll the crepe tightly, jelly-roll fashion. Cut the roll crosswise into 3 or 4 pieces. Tie each piece with a chive, if using. Repeat until all the crepes and filling are used. Wrap and refrigerate until serving time (up to 24 hours). Serve chilled.

Makes 45 to 60.

▪ *Spinach-Ham Fingers*

ONION BITES

These creamy, crunchy, easy-to-make bites are definitely adult fare!

32 narrow green onions
4 ounces cream cheese, chilled
4 ounces finely shredded sharp yellow
  Cheddar cheese (1 cup)

Wash and trim the onions, then dry with paper towels. Cut the green ends off so all the onions are about 4 inches long. With your hands, cover the white end of each onion with 1 to 1½ teaspoons of cream cheese. Roll the cream cheese-covered end of each onion in the Cheddar cheese. Cover and refrigerate for up to 8 hours. Serve chilled.

Makes 32.

NOTE: If the onions are limp, refresh them before trimming off the roots by placing the root ends in water for 10 minutes. Shake off the water, wrap them in plastic wrap, and refrigerate for at least 2 hours.

▪ *Onion Bites*

CREAM CHEESE BAR TRICKS

Try any or all of these quick tricks and watch them disappear at your next gathering. Plan to serve these at cocktail parties and on Super-Bowl Sunday.

FOR EACH TOPPING
1 package (8 ounces) cream cheese
  (let stand 30 minutes at room
  temperature)

For any of the topping options, place the cream cheese in the center of a shallow dish about 8 to 10 inches in diameter.

OPTION 1
1 cup salsa
Cilantro or parsley sprigs (optional)
Tortilla chips and celery sticks

Pour the salsa over the cream cheese; garnish with cilantro or parsley, if using. Serve with tortilla chips and celery.

OPTION 2
¾ cup chili sauce
¼ cup apple jelly
Chopped chives or green onions
  (optional)
Crackers or thick, crisp breadsticks

In a small saucepan, heat the chili sauce and jelly together until bubbly and the jelly melts; allow to cool. Pour the mixture over the cream cheese; garnish with chives or onions, if using. Serve with crackers or breadsticks.

YOGURT CHEESE–PIMIENTO SPREAD

Yogurt cheese is a wonderfully versatile low-fat item that you can use to top hot baked potatoes, spread on muffins, or any other way you'd use cream cheese. This spread is particularly beautiful when dolloped on endive spears or on wedges of green or red sweet pepper. It's also good on finger sandwiches, bagel chips, or crackers.

2 containers (8 ounces each) plain, low-fat yogurt (with no gelatin added)
8 ounces white Cheddar cheese, shredded, at room temperature (2 cups)
⅓ cup regular or reduced-fat mayonnaise
¼ cup finely chopped celery
1 jar (4 ounces) sliced pimiento, well-drained and coarsely chopped

TO MAKE YOGURT CHEESE: At least 2 to 5 days before serving, line a colander or strainer with 2 layers of 100% cotton cheesecloth. Place the yogurt in the lined colander and lay another piece of cheesecloth on top of the yogurt. Put the colander in a large bowl to catch the whey as it drips from the yogurt. Put the colander and bowl in the refrigerator and let it drain for 24 hours, pouring water from the bowl as needed, until the yogurt is thickened and reduced to 1 cup. Transfer the yogurt cheese to a small bowl, cover, and store in the refrigerator for up to five days.

In a medium bowl, beat together the yogurt cheese, Cheddar, and mayonnaise with an electric mixer until light and fluffy. Stir in the celery and pimientos. Cover and refrigerate until serving time.

Makes about 2¾ cups.

OPTION 3
1 cup pineapple preserves or apricot-pineapple preserves
2 teaspoons prepared horseradish
Green and red sweet pepper strips (optional)
Crackers or bagel chips

In a small bowl, stir together the preserves and horseradish. Pour the mixture over the cream cheese; garnish with peppers, if using. Serve with crackers or bagel chips.

■ *Cream Cheese Bar Trick (above); Yogurt Cheese-Pimiento Spread (right)*

OPTION 4
1 cup chutney
Orange slices and cherries (optional)
Crackers or crisp pita chips

Chop any large chunks in the chutney and pour it over the cream cheese. Garnish with oranges and cherries, if using. Serve with crackers or pita chips.

Each option makes about 24 servings.

BAKED CHICKEN NUGGETS WITH HONEY MUSTARD

No need to fry chicken nuggets when you can bake these crusty goodies. Serve on a buffet in a chafing dish, from an electric skillet set on low heat, or on a warm serving plate. Have toothpicks and a bowl of honey mustard nearby for dipping.

CHICKEN
8 skinless, boneless chicken breast halves
   (about 2 pounds)
1½ cups fine dry bread crumbs
1 teaspoon dried thyme, crushed
½ teaspoon salt
¼ teaspoon garlic powder
½ cup margarine or butter, melted

MUSTARD
½ cup brown mustard
¼ cup honey

TO MAKE THE CHICKEN: Preheat oven to 400°F. Cut the chicken into 1½-inch pieces. In a shallow bowl, mix together the bread crumbs, thyme, salt, and garlic powder. Dip the chicken pieces in butter, then roll them in the bread crumb mixture. Place on an ungreased baking sheet in a single layer. (Nuggets can be covered and refrigerated for up to 2 hours.) Bake for 20 minutes, or until brown and crisp and chicken is no longer pink. Serve hot.

TO MAKE THE MUSTARD: In a small bowl, mix together the mustard and honey. Serve as a dipping sauce for chicken nuggets.

Makes 10 to 12 servings.

CHILI CON QUESO

Serve this creamy, spicy dip in a fondue pot or small electric crockery cooker to keep it warm. A basket of tortilla chips and a container of sweet peppers, cauliflower flowerets, celery sticks, cherry tomatoes, and green onions are colorful accompaniments for Chili con Queso.

1 can (16 ounces) whole tomatoes
1 tablespoon cooking oil
1 large onion, finely chopped
2 cloves garlic, minced
1/2 teaspoon ground cumin
1/2 teaspoon dried oregano, crushed
1/4 teaspoon ground red pepper
1/2 cup coarsely chopped pimiento-stuffed green olives or pitted ripe olives
1 can (4 ounces) diced green chili peppers, drained
1 package (16 ounces) American cheese, cut into 1/2-inch cubes

Drain tomatoes, reserving the juice. Chop the tomatoes coarsely and set aside. In a large saucepan, heat the oil and cook the onions and garlic until tender, but not brown. Add the tomatoes, reserved tomato juice, cumin, oregano, and red pepper. Simmer, uncovered, over medium-low heat for 5 minutes.

Add the olives, chili peppers, and cheese. Cook over low heat, stirring often, until the cheese melts. Serve immediately or cover and refrigerate for up to 24 hours, then reheat to serve.

Makes 3½ cups.

NOTE: To reheat chilled dip, place in a microwave-safe dish. Cover and cook in a microwave oven on 100% power (HIGH) for 3 to 4 minutes or until heated through, stirring once every minute.

Chili con Queso (below); Baked Chicken Nuggets with Honey Mustard (left, bottom); Mrs. D's Bacon Breadstix (left, top)

▪ Christmas-in-California Soup

CHRISTMAS-IN-CALIFORNIA SOUP

Here's a wonderful cold soup that is sure to get oohs and aahs every time you serve it. The appetizing red and green colors make it especially appropriate for beginning a Christmas dinner.

TOMATO ICE

1 can (15 ounces) tomato puree
1/2 cup chicken broth
1 tablespoon lemon juice
1 teaspoon sugar
1/2 teaspoon bottled hot pepper sauce

SOUP

4 1/2 cups chicken broth
4 ripe avocados
3 tablespoons lemon juice
1 teaspoon ground cumin
1/2 cup finely chopped green onions
2 tablespoons finely chopped cilantro
1 tablespoon finely chopped, seeded jalapeño pepper
1/4 cup dairy sour cream
Salt, to taste
Chives or cilantro sprigs (optional)

TO MAKE THE TOMATO ICE: Up to 1 week before serving, mix together the tomato puree, broth, lemon juice, sugar, and hot pepper sauce. Pour into a shallow pan or ice-cube tray and freeze for 3 hours until firm but not solid. Transfer to a blender container or food processor bowl and blend or process until smooth. Return to freezer and freeze for at least 2 hours or up to 1 week.

TO MAKE THE SOUP: Early on the day of serving, heat the broth just to simmering. Meanwhile, seed and peel the avocados. In a medium bowl, mash the avocados with the lemon juice and cumin. Whisk in the heated broth. Stir in the onions, chopped cilantro, and jalapeño. In a blender container or food processor bowl (in 2 batches, if necessary), puree the mixture. Pour into a large bowl and whisk in the sour cream and salt. Cover and refrigerate until cold, about 2 hours.

TO SERVE: Ladle the soup into chilled soup bowls. Top each with several small scoops or spoonfuls of tomato ice and chives or cilantro, if using.

Makes 12 servings.

TEXAS CAVIAR

Straight from the heart of Texas, this chunky dip tastes great loaded on tortilla chips, or served as a salad on shredded lettuce.

2 cans (15 ounces each) black-eyed peas, drained and rinsed
1 can (15 ounces) hominy or garbanzo beans, drained and rinsed
2 tomatoes, seeded and chopped
4 green onions, coarsely chopped, including some green
2 cloves garlic, minced
1 green pepper, chopped
1 jalapeño pepper, seeded and finely chopped
1/2 cup chopped parsley
1/2 cup chopped cilantro
1 bottle (8 ounces) Italian salad dressing

In a large bowl, stir together the black-eyed peas, hominy or garbanzo beans, tomatoes, onions, garlic, green pepper, jalapeño pepper, parsley, and cilantro. Pour salad dressing over all; cover and refrigerate for at least 2 hours and up to 24 hours. Serve as a salad, or drain well and transfer to a serving bowl to use as a dip. Serve chilled.

Makes 7 cups.

WINTER SOUP

This low-fat, vitamin-packed vegetable soup is smooth and creamy—an ideal canvas for garnishing. Decorate as suggested or create your own work of art.

GARNISH
Red, green, and yellow sweet pepper
Ground nutmeg

SOUP
2 medium baking potatoes, peeled
1 cup chopped celery hearts (light-colored stalks)
2 cups trimmed and chopped cauliflower
4 cups chicken broth
1 tablespoon cooking oil
1/2 cup chopped onion
1 clove garlic, minced
1/2 teaspoon salt
1/8 teaspoon white pepper

TO PREPARE THE GARNISH: Cut sweet peppers in half and remove stems, seeds, and membranes. With a canapé cutter or tiny cookie cutter, cut shapes from the peppers. Or, cut shapes or strips with a sharp knife. Wrap in damp paper towels then plastic wrap and refrigerate until serving time.

TO MAKE THE SOUP: Up to 24 hours before serving, cut the potatoes into 1- to 2-inch pieces. In a large, covered saucepan, simmer the potatoes, celery, and cauliflower in the broth until very tender, about 20 to 30 minutes.

Meanwhile, heat the oil in a small skillet. Cook and stir the onion and garlic until very tender but not brown. Stir into the vegetable mixture. Stir in salt and pepper.

Let the soup cool slightly. Working in small batches, place the soup in a blender container; cover and blend until smooth. Return to saucepan; heat just to simmering and serve immediately, or refrigerate for up to 24 hours and reheat gently before serving.

Garnish with sweet pepper cutouts or a sprinkling of ground nutmeg.

Makes 10 to 12 servings.

▪ *Texas Caviar (left); Winter Soup (above)*

Better Homes and Gardens®
'Tis the Season
Food Safety Update

Due to USDA information received since the printing of this book regarding recipes for uncooked pickles, such as the <u>Refrigerator Pickles recipe on page 87</u>, a new method for this recipe has been tested in the Better Homes and Gardens® Test Kitchen. Please insert the following procedure for the recipe printed in this book:

> Wash cucumbers and thinly slice. In a Dutch oven combine vinegar, sugar, dill, pickling spice, peppers, and garlic, if using. Bring to a full boil. Add cucumbers. Return to boiling, stirring occasionally. Remove from heat and cool. Spoon pickles and juice into a clean 1-gallon glass jar with a tight-fitting lid. Cover the jar first with plastic wrap, then with the lid. Refrigerate for up to 1 month.

> (*Note: 1 tablespoon dried dillweed may be substituted for the fresh dillweed.)

WATERCRESS SOUP

This beautiful, healthful soup is flecked with peppery watercress. Set aside six perfect watercress sprigs for garnish, if you like.

GARNISH (OPTIONAL)
1 carrot
6 watercress sprigs

SOUP
1 cup shredded carrots
1 cup snipped watercress
1/2 cup water
3 tablespoons margarine or butter
3 tablespoons all-purpose flour
1 teaspoon salt
1/2 to 1 teaspoon curry powder
3 cups milk

TO PREPARE THE GARNISH: Up to 24 hours before serving, peel carrot and cut several small pieces for each serving. Wrap carrot and watercress sprigs in damp paper towels and plastic wrap. Refrigerate.

TO MAKE THE SOUP: Up to 24 hours before serving, in a small saucepan, bring carrots, watercress, and water to a boil. Cover, reduce heat, and simmer for 10 minutes. (Do not drain.) Allow to cool slightly; puree in a blender container or food processor bowl, stopping and pushing down as necessary.

In a medium saucepan over medium heat, melt the margarine or butter. Stir in the flour, salt, and curry powder. Stir until thick and bubbly. Gradually stir in the milk and cook, stirring often, until the mixture is smooth and slightly thickened. Cook and stir 2 minutes more. Whisk the vegetable puree into the milk mixture. Serve immediately or cover and refrigerate for up to 24 hours, then reheat before serving. If necessary, thin with additional milk. Garnish each serving, if using, with carrot pieces and a watercress sprig.

Makes 6 servings.

REFRIGERATOR PICKLES

In Denmark, these sweet, limp pickle slices are served as a relish with nearly every lunch and dinner menu. If desired, tie the pickling spice, peppers, and garlic in a 100% cotton cheesecloth bag so they can be easily removed.

4 pounds small cucumbers (peel if skins are waxed)
1 quart white vinegar
3 cups sugar
1/2 cup chopped fresh dillweed
1 tablespoon mixed pickling spice
1 tablespoon whole black peppers
8 cloves garlic, sliced (optional)

Slice cucumbers thinly and place in a clean, 1-gallon glass jar with a tight-fitting lid. In a large bowl, stir together the vinegar, sugar, dill, pickling spice, peppers, and garlic, if using. (Sugar may not completely dissolve.) Pour over the cucumbers. Cover the jar first with plastic wrap, then with the lid. Refrigerate at least 3 days, shaking the jar once a day for the first 3 days. Store in the refrigerator for up to 1 month.

Makes about 1 gallon.

■ *Watercress Soup (left); Refrigerator Pickles (below)*

CHAPTER 2

Entrées for Dinners and Buffets

EVERY SHOW NEEDS A STAR AND, IN GALA HOLIDAY DINNERS AND BUFFET MENUS, THE ENTRÉE IS THE LEAD AND THE OTHER DISHES ARE THE SUPPORTING CAST. A DINNER STARRING A GOLDEN ROAST TURKEY IS A SURE SHOW-STOPPER—ESPECIALLY ONE ACCOMPANIED BY APPLE-ONION STUFFING, SWEET POTATOES, AND CRANBERRY SAUCE.

LESS FORMAL ENTERTAINING MAY FEATURE A DELICIOUS DEEP-DISH LASAGNA WITH SALAD AND BREADSTICKS OR VEGETABLE-STUFFED VEGETABLES SERVED ALONGSIDE STEAMED ZUCCHINI AND CARROTS AND SWEET-AND-SOUR RED CABBAGE.

WHATEVER YOU SERVE, GUESTS ARE SURE TO REMEMBER THE GRACIOUS WARMTH OF YOUR HOME.

ROLLED RIB ROAST WITH MAKE-AHEAD POPOVERS

A fragrant, generous beef roast is a rare treat. Crusty, airy popovers are an ideal accompaniment for the roast, along with fried potatoes and steamed zucchini and carrots. If you use custard cups for large popovers, you'll need to make two recipes of popovers to have enough for one popover per serving. You can bake and freeze them for up to a month before serving.

POPOVERS

2 eggs
1 cup milk
1 cup all-purpose flour
2 tablespoons finely chopped parsley
1/4 teaspoon salt
Dash of ground nutmeg
2 tablespoons finely shredded Parmesan cheese

ROAST

1 boneless beef rib roast (4 1/2 to 5 pounds)

GRAVY

2 tablespoons margarine or butter, softened
2 or 3 tablespoons all-purpose flour
1/2 cup dry red or white wine or water
Salt and pepper, to taste

TO MAKE THE POPOVERS: Generously grease ten 2 1/2" muffin cups or six 6-ounce custard cups.

Preheat the oven to 400°F. In a large bowl, beat the eggs lightly. Add the milk, flour, parsley, salt, and nutmeg; beat just until smooth (do not overbeat). Fill muffin cups 3/4 full or custard cups 1/2 full. (If cups are over-filled, the popovers will be heavy.) Sprinkle with cheese. Bake about 40 minutes until golden brown and very firm. Immediately after removing from oven, prick each with a fork to allow steam to escape. Remove from the cups and serve warm, or allow to cool completely, wrap in flexible airtight freezer wrap, date, and freeze for up to 1 month. To reheat, remove from the freezer wrap and heat, uncovered, in a 350°F oven on an ungreased baking sheet for 10 to 15 minutes.

TO MAKE THE ROAST: Preheat the oven to 350°F. Place the meat, fat side up, on a rack in a shallow roasting pan. Do not cover or add liquid. Insert a meat thermometer so it reaches the center of the roast. For medium-rare (150°F), roast for 1 3/4 to 2 1/4 hours; for medium (160°F), roast for 2 1/4 to 2 1/2 hours.

Remove to serving platter and let rest 15 minutes before carving. (If you froze the popovers, place them in the oven to heat now.)

TO MAKE THE GRAVY: In small bowl, stir together margarine or butter and flour. Pour juices from roasting pan into a heat-proof measuring cup. Spoon the fat off the top and discard. Measure the remaining juices and add 1/2 cup wine or water and enough additional water to make 2 cups. Return juices to the roasting pan and place on the stovetop over medium heat, stirring to scrape up browned bits. Add the butter and flour mixture to the juices; cook and stir until the sauce begins to thicken and bubble; cook and stir 1 minute more. Season to taste with salt and pepper. Pour into a gravy boat and serve with the roast.

Makes 10 to 12 servings.

NOTE: For thinner gravy, use 2 tablespoons flour; for slightly thicker gravy, use 3 tablespoons flour.

■ *Rolled Rib Roast with Make-Ahead Popovers*

ROAST TURKEY WITH APPLE-ONION STUFFING

Turkey has become an everyday staple for many Americans, but it's still a holiday masterpiece when presented on a beautifully garnished platter along with fragrant stuffing and giblet gravy. The size and length of cooking time for roasting a turkey may daunt a novice cook, but take heart. Just follow these instructions and you'll produce a golden, succulent turkey to impress your family and guests.

TURKEY
1 turkey (12 to 14 pounds)

STUFFING
12 cups dry or fresh ½-inch bread cubes
¾ cup margarine or butter
1½ cups chopped onions
1 cup finely chopped celery
2 teaspoons dried thyme, crushed
2 teaspoons dried marjoram, crushed
1½ teaspoons ground sage
3 cups peeled, cored, and chopped Granny Smith apples
¼ to ½ cup chicken broth
1 teaspoon salt
¾ cup raisins (optional)
Cooking oil or melted unsalted butter

GRAVY
Drippings from roasting pan
¼ cup all-purpose flour
Salt and white pepper, to taste

TO PREPARE THE TURKEY: If turkey is frozen, thaw the wrapped turkey in a shallow baking dish in the refrigerator (allow about 2½ days). Remove giblets, rinse turkey inside and out, and pat dry with paper towels. Place the giblets in a medium saucepan, cover with 2 cups water, and, while the turkey roasts, simmer over low heat for about 1 hour until tender. Drain and reserve the cooking liquid. Finely chop the giblets and refrigerate giblets and cooking liquid until needed to make gravy.

TO MAKE THE STUFFING: If using fresh bread cubes, spread them in a single layer in a 15½" x 10½" x 2" baking pan. Bake in a 300°F oven 10 to 15 minutes, or until dry, stirring twice. Or, let stand, loosely covered, at room temperature for 8 to 12 hours. Place the bread cubes in a very large mixing bowl. In a large skillet, melt the margarine or butter; add the onions and celery and cook until nearly tender. Add the thyme, marjoram, and sage; mix thoroughly. Add the apples and continue cooking until the apples are tender. Pour over the bread cubes. Sprinkle with ¼ cup of the broth and salt. Add raisins, if using. Add more broth if you like moister stuffing. Toss with 2 forks or wooden spoons until thoroughly mixed.

Preheat the oven to 325°F. Stuff the neck cavity of the turkey first and secure the skin to the back with a metal skewer. Turn the wings under the body. Lightly stuff the large cavity—the stuffing will expand as it heats. (If you have extra stuffing, place it in a lightly greased casserole and refrigerate until 1 hour before turkey is done.) Secure the legs by slipping them under the skin flap under the legs, or tie the legs together, then to the tail with kitchen twine.

Place the turkey on a rack in a large shallow roasting pan (about 2 inches deep). Insert a meat thermometer into the center of one of the inside thigh muscles, not touching the bone. Rub the turkey thoroughly with oil or butter.

Roast the turkey until the meat thermometer registers 180° to 185°F (about 4½ to 5 hours). Check the bird after about 2 hours, covering loosely with foil when the skin is golden brown, to prevent it from overbrowning. The leg will move very freely when the turkey is done. (If you have extra stuffing in a casserole, put it in the oven, covered, with the turkey for the last hour of roasting.) Remove the turkey from the oven, carefully transfer it to a serving platter, and keep it covered loosely with foil for 15 minutes before carving.

TO MAKE THE GRAVY: Pour the drippings from the roasting pan into a heat-proof measuring cup. Spoon the fat off the top and measure out ¼ cup of the fat. Measure the remaining juices and add the giblet cooking liquid, if needed, to equal 2 cups; set aside.

In a medium saucepan over medium heat, stir together the reserved fat from turkey drippings and flour until bubbly. Add the measured juices all at once; cook and stir constantly, until thickened and bubbly. Reduce the heat and cook and stir 1 to 2 minutes more. Add the chopped giblets and heat thoroughly. Taste for seasoning and add salt and pepper, if needed. Pour into a gravy boat and serve.

Makes 8 to 10 servings.

NOTE: As you work with the raw turkey, wash all equipment and surfaces that come in contact with the turkey or juices.

Immediately after dinner, prepare leftovers for refrigeration. Remove every bit of stuffing from inside the turkey and, if you like, cut the turkey from the bones. Wrap and refrigerate the turkey, stuffing, and gravy separately. Serve within 1 to 2 days and heat thoroughly before serving.

▪ *Roast Turkey with Apple-Onion Stuffing (left)*

EASY-BAKE PORK CHOPS

Bill takes gorgeous pictures—and he cooks. This simple preparation (Bill's specialty) results in juicy, tender chops. Serve them with steamed new potatoes, carrots and green beans, and crusty bread.

4 pork chops (1-inch thick)
1 tablespoon olive oil
$1/2$ to $3/4$ cup fine dry bread crumbs (seasoned or plain)

Preheat the oven to 350°F. Trim all visible fat from the pork chops and discard it. Rub the chops with the oil; set aside. Pour the bread crumbs onto a plate and pat the chops into the crumbs until very well covered. Place the chops on a rack in a shallow roasting pan and bake for 45 minutes, or until the juices run clear. Serve immediately.

Makes 4 servings.

NATHANA'S BAKED HAM

Nathana Josephs is an extraordinary cook, and this shiny brown baked ham is often the centerpiece of her buffet table.

1 bone-in fully cooked ham, shank portion (5 to 7 pounds)
Whole cloves
1 cup firmly packed brown sugar
3 tablespoons brown mustard
3 tablespoons orange or pineapple juice

Preheat the oven to 325°F. Remove and discard the tough skin from the ham, leaving a thin layer of fat. With a sharp knife, make $1/8$-inch-deep diagonal cuts (in 2 directions) into the fat, being careful not to cut into the meat. Insert whole cloves into the center of each diamond-shape created by the diagonal cuts. Place the ham on a rack in a shallow baking pan. Do not cover or add liquid. Insert a meat thermometer into the thickest part of the ham, but not touching the bone.

In a small saucepan, mix together the brown sugar, mustard, and juice. Cook and stir over medium heat until combined and the sugar dissolves. Brush the sugar mixture over the ham.

Bake the ham for 2 to $2^{1/2}$ hours, or until the meat thermometer registers 140°F, basting with the sugar mixture every 30 minutes. Serve hot, slicing after allowing the ham to rest for 15 minutes.

Makes 10 to 12 servings.

▪ *Nathana's Baked Ham, Stuffed Tomatoes, Orange Brussels Sprouts, and a selection of quick breads*

SHRIMP (OR CHICKEN) GRUYÈRE CREPES

This classy, creamy casserole is perfect for a brunch or light dinner. Make the crepes and freeze them up to one month ahead, then assemble the dish a day before serving. Let the chilled casserole heat, covered, in a 350°F oven for 35 to 40 minutes or until bubbly while you chat with your guests. The aroma wafting from the kitchen will tell your friends that something wonderful is on its way! This recipe can be halved for a smaller group.

CREPES
1 cup milk
1 cup all-purpose flour
4 eggs, lightly beaten
2 tablespoons cold water
2 tablespoons cooking oil
1/2 teaspoon salt

SAUCE
3/4 cup margarine or butter
3/4 cup all-purpose flour
3 1/2 cups milk
12 ounces Gruyère or Swiss cheese, shredded (3 cups)
2 teaspoons tomato paste
2 teaspoons lemon juice
1/2 teaspoon ground white pepper
2 tablespoons margarine or butter
2 tablespoons finely chopped red sweet pepper
2 tablespoons finely chopped green pepper
8 ounces fresh mushrooms, cleaned and sliced
3 cups chopped cooked shrimp or chicken

■ *Shrimp Gruyère Crepes*

To make the crepes: In a medium bowl, combine the milk, flour, eggs, water, oil, and salt. Beat with a rotary beater until well-mixed.

Heat a lightly greased 6-inch skillet over medium heat for 1 minute. Stir the batter and pour 2 tablespoons into the skillet. Immediately swirl the skillet so the batter covers the bottom of the skillet—the crepe will be very thin. Let it cook for about 30 seconds until it just begins to brown on the bottom. Invert skillet over a paper towel-lined baking sheet and remove crepe. Continue cooking crepes until all the batter is used, for about 20 crepes. Use immediately or let them cool, then stack with waxed paper between each crepe. Wrap the stack with flexible freezer wrap or foil, label, and freeze for up to 1 month. To thaw, unwrap and leave at room temperature for about an hour.

To make the sauce: In a large saucepan over medium heat, melt 3/4 cup margarine or butter. Stir in the flour and heat until bubbly. Add the milk and stir until the sauce is thick and bubbly. Add the cheese and stir until it melts. Stir in the tomato paste, lemon juice, and white pepper; set aside. In a small skillet, melt the 2 tablespoons margarine or butter and cook the peppers and mushrooms until tender. Drain and add to the cheese sauce. Remove 1 cup of sauce and stir in the shrimp or chicken.

To fill the crepes: Place crepes on a flat surface and put about 2 tablespoons of shrimp or chicken mixture just off-center in each. Roll the crepes and place them, seam side down, into 2 lightly greased 3-quart rectangular baking dishes (about 10 crepes in each dish).

Pour the remaining cheese sauce over the rolled crepes. Bake, covered, in a 350°F oven for 25 to 30 minutes, or until bubbly.

Makes 10 servings.

FELIZ NAVIDAD TACO CASSEROLE

This Mexican-style casserole is *muy bien* and can be made a day ahead and heated just before serving. It goes together easily, so if you're serving a crowd, make more than one at a time.

2 cans (14 1/2 ounces each) whole tomatoes, drained
2 cloves garlic, minced
2 tablespoons finely chopped cilantro
2 tablespoons cooking oil
1 cup chopped onion
2 cans (4 ounces each) diced green chili peppers, drained
2 containers (8 ounces each) dairy sour cream
1/4 cup all-purpose flour
1/3 cup milk
12 corn tortillas (6-inch)
2 cups shredded cooked chicken
8 ounces *queso blanco* or Monterey Jack cheese, shredded or crumbled (2 cups)

Lightly grease a 3-quart rectangular baking dish. In a blender container or food processor bowl, blend or process tomatoes, garlic, and cilantro just until chunky; set aside. In a large skillet, heat the oil over medium heat and cook onion until tender but not brown. Mix onion and chili peppers into tomato mixture. In a small bowl, blend together the sour cream, flour, and milk; set aside.

Warm a third of the tortillas at a time in the microwave oven on 100% power (HIGH) for 30 seconds, or wrap all the tortillas in foil and heat at 350°F for 15 minutes. Quarter the tortillas. Spread a third of the tortilla pieces over the bottom of the baking dish. Layer half the chicken, a third of the tomato sauce, a

1 teaspoon dried oregano, crushed
1 teaspoon dried basil, crushed
1/2 teaspoon fennel seeds, crushed
Dash of ground nutmeg
1 package (8 ounces) lasagna noodles
2 eggs, lightly beaten
1 container (16 ounces) cottage cheese or (15 ounces) ricotta cheese
1/2 cup finely shredded Parmesan cheese
1 package (10 ounces) frozen chopped spinach, thawed and well-drained
1/2 cup finely shredded carrots
1/3 cup finely chopped parsley
16 ounces sliced mozzarella cheese

In a large skillet, heat the oil and cook the onion, pepper, and garlic until the onion is tender. Stir in the tomatoes (with juice), tomato paste, bay leaf, oregano, basil, fennel seeds, and nutmeg. Simmer, covered, stirring occasionally, for 20 to 30 minutes. Remove and discard the bay leaf.

Meanwhile, cook the lasagna noodles in 4 quarts boiling water for 12 minutes. Drain and rinse in cold water to stop the cooking process; set aside.

In a medium bowl, mix together the eggs, cottage or ricotta cheese, Parmesan, spinach, carrots, and parsley; set aside.

Preheat the oven to 350°F. Pour 1/2 cup of the tomato mixture into a 3-quart rectangular baking dish. Top with a third of the lasagna noodles, a third of the cheese mixture, and a third of the mozzarella slices. Repeat the layers twice. Top with the remaining tomato sauce. (At this point, the casserole may be covered and refrigerated for up to 24 hours.)

Bake, covered, for 40 to 45 minutes, or until bubbly. (If chilled, bake, covered, for 1 hour.) Let stand 10 minutes before cutting.

Makes 8 servings.

---

third of the sour cream mixture, and a third of the cheese; repeat the layers again. Top with the remaining tortillas, sauce, sour cream mixture, and cheese. Bake, uncovered, at 350°F for 35 to 40 minutes, or until heated through. Or, cover and refrigerate for up to 24 hours. Bake, covered, for 15 minutes, then uncover and bake for 25 to 30 minutes, or until heated through.

Makes 8 servings.

▪ Feliz Navidad *Taco Casserole (above)*; *Deep-Dish Lasagna (right)*

DEEP-DISH LASAGNA

As a friend once said, "Lasagna is one of those things we never get enough of in one lifetime." Serve this scrumptious meatless lasagna on a buffet table and invite your friends to have as much as they want. To go with the lasagna, create a self-serve salad bar that includes mixed greens, chick-peas, sweet peppers, and a choice of dressings.

1 tablespoon cooking or olive oil
1/2 cup chopped onion
1/3 cup chopped green pepper
2 cloves garlic, minced
1 can (14 1/2 ounces) whole tomatoes, cut up (with juice)
1 can (6 ounces) tomato paste
1 bay leaf

VEGETABLE-STUFFED VEGETABLES

You can make this dish especially for vegetarian guests—they'll love you for it. These vegetables are so good, in fact, your meat-eating friends and family will enjoy them, too. Serve them with poached apple or pear slices and steamed broccoli.

4 small acorn squash (12 to 16 ounces each) or 4 large green peppers

¹⁄₂ cup chopped onion

¹⁄₂ cup chopped celery

¹⁄₂ teaspoon ground sage

¹⁄₄ teaspoon dried thyme, crushed

2 tablespoons margarine or butter

1 jar (4¹⁄₂ ounces) sliced mushrooms, drained

About 1 cup (half of a 19-ounce can) cannellini or white kidney beans, drained and rinsed

¹⁄₂ cup water or vegetable broth

1 teaspoon soy sauce

3 cups dry whole-wheat bread cubes

¹⁄₂ cup chopped hazelnuts or sunflower seeds

6 ounces shredded Cheddar cheese (1¹⁄₂ cups)

For squash, halve each lengthwise and remove the seeds and fiber. Place the squash, cut side down, in a shallow baking dish. Bake in a 350°F oven for 30 minutes. For peppers, halve each lengthwise and remove the seeds and membrane. Immerse the peppers in boiling water for 3 minutes. Invert onto paper towels to drain well.

Meanwhile, in a large skillet, cook the onion, celery, sage, and thyme in the margarine or butter until the onion is tender. Remove from the heat and stir in the mush-rooms, beans, water or broth, and soy sauce. Put the bread cubes and nuts or seeds in a large bowl and, with 2 forks, toss the vegetable mixture with the bread until well-mixed.

Place the halved squash or peppers, cut side up, in a large, shallow baking dish. Evenly divide the stuffing among the halves (about ¹⁄₂ cup in each). Cover the dish tightly with foil. Bake 20 minutes, or until heated through and squash or peppers are tender. Remove the foil, sprinkle with the cheese, and bake an additional 5 minutes.

Makes 8 servings.

NOTE: To make dry bread cubes for stuffing, cut bread into ¹⁄₂-inch cubes. Use 4 to 6 slices of bread for 3 cups of dry cubes. Spread the cubes in a single layer in a shallow baking pan. Bake in a 300°F oven for 10 to 15 minutes, or until dry; stir twice. Or, let the cubes stand, loosely covered, at room temperature for 8 to 12 hours.

▪ *Vegetable-Stuffed Vegetables (left)*

QUICK-MIX RELISHES

QUICK VEGGIE RELISH
In a food processor bowl fitted with a metal blade, process ¹⁄₂ cup each coarsely chopped red radishes and zucchini and 1 cup chopped iceberg lettuce with 2 tablespoons white vinegar, 2 tablespoons granulated sugar, ¹⁄₄ teaspoon salt, and ¹⁄₄ teaspoon celery seed, with on/off turns until the vegetables are minced. Transfer to a bowl and let stand at least 15 minutes or up to 1 hour. Drain and serve. Makes about 1¹⁄₄ cups.

QUICK PICKLED BEETS WITH CARAWAY
Drain a 16-ounce can of small whole or sliced beets and place beets in a heatproof bowl. Add ¹⁄₃ cup heated cider vinegar, 2 tablespoons sugar, and 2 teaspoons caraway seeds, crushed. Chill 6 to 24 hours, stirring occasionally. Drain before serving. Makes about 1³⁄₄ cups.

QUICK SALSA
In a food processor bowl or blender container, combine a 14¹⁄₂-ounce can of whole tomatoes, drained; 1 medium onion, cut up; ¹⁄₃ cup loosely packed cilantro; ¹⁄₂ teaspoon dried oregano; ¹⁄₂ teaspoon ground cumin; ¹⁄₄ teaspoon salt; and ¹⁄₈ teaspoon ground red pepper. Cover and process or blend just until the vegetables are coarsely chopped (do not puree). Makes about 1¹⁄₄ cups.

CHAPTER 3

Holiday Side Dishes

WHEN PLANNING YOUR SPECIAL HOLIDAY MENUS—WHETHER FOR FAMILY MEALS OR FESTIVE SPECTACULARS—CONSIDER COLOR AND CONTRAST. FOODS THAT ARE SMOOTH AND CRUNCHY, BLAND AND SPICY, BEIGE AND COLORFUL CAN ALL BE SERVED IN A MEAL THAT WILL APPEAL TO BOTH THE EYE AND THE PALATE.

THE SIDE DISHES IN THIS SECTION WILL INSPIRE YOU WITH WAYS TO GIVE YOUR MEALS A SPARK WITH SUCH BRIGHT SPOTS AS PERKY ORANGE BRUSSELS SPROUTS, CREAMY BROCCOLI-CHEESE BAKE, COLORFUL PECAN-CRUSTED SWEET POTATOES, AND CRUNCHY ORANGE-RED ONION SALAD WITH MIXED GREENS.

OVEN-BAKED SPANISH RICE

When you're baking a casserole or bread for dinner and the oven is on, go ahead and bake this colorful, well-seasoned rice dish, too.

2 tablespoons cooking oil or olive oil
1 cup chopped onion
1 cup chopped green pepper
1 clove garlic, minced
1 cup uncooked long-grain rice
1 teaspoon ground cumin
1/2 teaspoon dried oregano, crushed
1/2 teaspoon chili powder
2 cans (16 ounces each) diced tomatoes
1 1/4 cups water
1 small bay leaf
1 teaspoon salt
1/2 teaspoon sugar
1/4 teaspoon pepper

Preheat the oven to 350°F. Lightly grease a 2-quart casserole; set aside. (If your casserole is flame-proof, you can prepare the recipe in the casserole instead of a skillet on the stovetop, then place the casserole in the oven to bake.)

In a large skillet or a flame-proof casserole, heat the oil over medium-low heat and cook the onion, green pepper, and garlic until tender. Add the rice, cumin, oregano, and chili powder. Stir until the rice begins to turn golden. Add the tomatoes (with juice), water, bay leaf, salt, sugar, and pepper; stir well. Pour the rice mixture into the prepared casserole. Cover tightly with foil and bake for 35 to 40 minutes, or until the rice is tender. Remove and discard the bay leaf.

Makes 8 servings.

BROCCOLI-CHEESE BAKE

Serve this substantial side dish with broiled meat or poultry or feature it as an entrée for brunch or a light supper. Stir in three slices of cooked and crumbled bacon or 1/2 cup chopped ham with the rice, if you like.

1 tablespoon cooking oil or olive oil
4 green onions, trimmed and thinly sliced (including some green) (1/2 cup)
1 clove garlic, minced
3 eggs
3 cups cooked brown or long-grain white rice
1 package (10 ounces) frozen chopped broccoli, thawed and drained
2 cups milk
4 ounces shredded Swiss cheese (1 cup)
1/4 cup chopped parsley
3/4 teaspoon salt
1/4 teaspoon ground nutmeg

Preheat the oven to 350°F. Lightly grease a 2-quart rectangular baking dish; set aside. In a small saucepan, heat the oil over medium-low heat. Add the onions and garlic; cook until tender. In a large bowl, beat the eggs lightly and add the cooked rice, onion mixture, broccoli, milk, cheese, parsley, salt, and nutmeg. Stir until well-combined. Transfer to the prepared baking dish and bake, uncovered, about 45 minutes, or until set.

Makes 6 servings.

■ *Broccoli-Cheese Bake (above)*

STUFFED TOMATOES

These tomatoes, stuffed with flavor, add color and interest to many menus. Serve accompanied by steamed broccoli along with pot roast, lamb chops, baked chicken, or Easy-Bake Pork Chops (see page 94).

4 tomatoes
Sugar or salt (optional)
4 slices bacon, cut into ½-inch pieces
½ cup chopped onion
1 tablespoon snipped parsley
1 teaspoon dried oregano, crushed
¼ cup grated Parmesan cheese
2 cups soft white or whole-wheat bread
   crumbs

Preheat the oven to 350°F. Lightly grease a 13" x 9" baking pan; set aside. Cut the tomatoes in half crosswise. Carefully remove the seeds and pulp with a spoon. Discard the seeds but reserve 1 cup of the pulp. Sprinkle the inside of each tomato half with sugar or salt, if using. Put the tomato halves, cut side up, in the baking pan.

In a large skillet, cook the bacon until crisp. Remove and drain on paper towels, then crumble and set aside. Pour off all but 1 tablespoon of drippings from the skillet. Add the onion and cook until tender. Add the parsley, oregano, and reserved tomato pulp; stir until hot. Remove from the heat and add the bacon, Parmesan, and bread crumbs; stir thoroughly.

Carefully fill each tomato half with the bread mixture (about ¼ cup in each half). Bake, uncovered, 20 minutes, or until tender and heated through.

Makes 8 servings.

▪ *Stuffed Tomatoes*

CHEESE GRITS

If you've never tried grits, the name may put you off. But once you've tried them, you'll be hooked on this corn-derived grain that is a delicious side dish for ham and eggs, baked fish, or vegetable stews.

3½ cups water
½ teaspoon salt
1 cup quick-cooking grits
4 ounces shredded Cheddar cheese (1 cup)
¼ cup margarine or butter
¼ cup milk
2 eggs, beaten

Preheat the oven to 350°F. Lightly grease a 2-quart square baking dish. Bring the water and salt to a boil in a medium saucepan. Slowly stir the grits into the water and simmer, uncovered, about 10 minutes, stirring frequently, until thick. Remove the grits from the heat and add the cheese, margarine or butter, milk, and eggs. Mix well. Pour into the prepared dish and bake, uncovered, 35 minutes, or until set. Let stand 10 minutes before serving.

Makes 6 servings.

PECAN-CRUSTED SWEET POTATOES

Sweet potatoes are very nutritious, but your family and guests won't be thinking about that while they enjoy these luscious potatoes.

POTATOES
4 sweet potatoes (about 1½ pounds) or 1 can (23 ounces) sweet potatoes, drained
⅓ cup milk

¼ cup orange juice
2 tablespoons margarine or butter, melted
4 eggs
2 tablespoons brown sugar
1 teaspoon baking powder
½ teaspoon ground cinnamon
½ teaspoon ground ginger
¼ teaspoon ground mace
¼ teaspoon salt

TOPPING
1 cup coarsely chopped pecans
⅓ cup firmly packed brown sugar
3 tablespoons margarine or butter, melted

TO MAKE THE POTATOES: Preheat the oven to 325°F. Lightly grease a 2-quart casserole or soufflé dish; set aside. If using fresh sweet potatoes, wash, peel, and cut off the woody portions and ends. Cut into quarters or cubes. Cook, covered, in enough salted boiling water to cover for 25 to 35 minutes, or until tender. Drain.

In a large bowl, mash the cooked or canned potatoes (should have about 2⅓ cups); add the milk, orange juice, margarine or butter, eggs, brown sugar, baking powder, cinnamon, ginger, mace, and salt. Mix by hand or with an electric mixer until smooth and fluffy. Spoon into the prepared baking dish.

TO MAKE THE TOPPING: In a small bowl, mix together the pecans, brown sugar, and margarine or butter. Spoon evenly over the sweet potato mixture. (At this point, the dish may be covered and refrigerated for up to 24 hours.) Bake, uncovered, 40 minutes, or until puffed and the topping is golden brown. (If chilled, bake about 50 minutes.)

Makes 6 to 8 servings.

■ *Cheese Grits*

MINNESOTA WILD RICE

The long brown grains of wild rice cook to a satisfying crunchy texture and a grainy flavor that especially complements game, chicken, turkey, and duck.

1¼ cups wild rice (8 ounces)
1 tablespoon instant beef or vegetable
  bouillon granules
3 cups water
¼ cup margarine or butter
1 pound fresh mushrooms, cleaned and sliced
2 tablespoons lemon juice
2 tablespoons finely chopped parsley
2 tablespoons finely chopped onion
1 cup chopped pecans

Rinse the rice in water until the water runs clear. Add the rice and bouillon granules to the water in a large saucepan or 4½-quart Dutch oven. Bring to boiling, cover, and reduce the heat. Simmer for 40 minutes, or until the rice is tender. Drain, if necessary.

Meanwhile, in a large skillet, melt the margarine or butter over medium-low heat. Add the mushrooms; cook and stir until tender. Sprinkle with the lemon juice.

Stir the mushrooms, parsley, onion, and pecans into the drained, cooked rice. Serve immediately.

Makes 10 to 12 servings.

■ *Minnesota Wild Rice*

CORN STUFFING BALLS

Just about everybody loves stuffing, and this is a recipe you can use any time of year to satisfy that craving. Serve with baked poultry, ham steak, or pork chops. To serve as an entrée, mix in leftover cubed turkey or chicken and serve with gravy, cranberry sauce, and steamed vegetables.

¼ cup margarine or butter
1 cup chopped celery
½ cup chopped onion
1 can (15 ounces) cream-style corn
½ cup water
1½ teaspoons poultry seasoning
½ teaspoon salt
¼ teaspoon pepper
4 cups unseasoned toasted bread cubes
1 egg, lightly beaten
¼ cup margarine or butter, melted

Preheat the oven to 375°F. In a large skillet, melt ¼ cup margarine or butter and cook the celery and onion until tender. Add the corn, water, poultry seasoning, salt, and pepper. Bring to boil. Put the bread cubes in a large bowl. Add the corn mixture and mix lightly. Let cool slightly, then thoroughly stir in the egg. Shape the mixture into 16 balls, using ¼ cup mixture for each. Place them in a large shallow baking dish. (At this point, the stuffing balls may be covered and refrigerated for up to 24 hours.) Before baking, pour ¼ cup melted margarine or butter over all the balls. Bake, uncovered, 18 to 20 minutes until golden brown. (If chilled, bake for 20 to 25 minutes.)

Makes 16.

■ *Corn Stuffing Balls (below); Orange Brussels Sprouts (right)*

ORANGE BRUSSELS SPROUTS

During the winter, some farmers' markets feature fresh brussels sprouts still on the stalk. Otherwise, they're often available in the supermarket produce department and always in the frozen vegetable section. They have a mild cabbagelike flavor and must be cooked thoroughly to be digestible.

1½ pounds fresh brussels sprouts or 2 packages (10 ounces each) frozen
1 tablespoon cornstarch
1 tablespoon sugar
2 teaspoons finely shredded orange peel
⅛ teaspoon ground cardamom
1 cup orange juice
2 tablespoons margarine or butter
1 orange, peeled, sectioned, and coarsely chopped

Prepare the fresh brussels sprouts by trimming off any withered leaves; cut an X in the stalk end of each. In a large saucepan, cook the fresh or frozen brussels sprouts, covered, in a small amount of lightly salted boiling water for 10 to 12 minutes, or until crisp-tender. Meanwhile, in a small saucepan, stir together the cornstarch, sugar, orange peel, and cardamom. Slowly stir in the orange juice and bring to a boil, stirring constantly, until thickened and bubbly. Cook and stir 2 minutes more. Stir in the margarine or butter and chopped oranges until heated through. Drain the brussels sprouts in a colander, then mix them in the orange sauce. Serve hot.

Makes about 10 servings.

CANDIED CARROTS AND PARSNIPS

Parsnips are a creamy white winter root vegetable with a sweet flavor that combines well with other vegetables. Here, they're simmered with carrots, then covered with a caramel-like glaze.

1 pound carrots, scraped, trimmed, and cut into 1$\frac{1}{2}$-inch julienne strips

1 pound small, young parsnips, scraped, trimmed, and cut into 1$\frac{1}{2}$-inch julienne strips (if the center tops are pithy, cut them out)

$\frac{1}{4}$ cup margarine or butter

$\frac{1}{2}$ cup firmly packed brown sugar

1 tablespoon lemon juice

$\frac{1}{2}$ teaspoon salt

$\frac{1}{4}$ teaspoon ground nutmeg

In a large saucepan, cook the carrots and parsnips, covered, in a small amount of boiling water for 8 to 10 minutes, or until crisp-tender.

Drain the vegetables in a colander and set aside. In the same saucepan, melt the margarine or butter. Stir in the brown sugar, lemon juice, salt, and nutmeg. Over low heat, stir until the sugar is melted. Return the carrots and parsnips to the pan. Stir to coat with the sugar mixture. Serve hot.

Makes 10 to 12 servings.

■ *Orange-Red Onion Salad with Mixed Greens*

ORANGE-RED ONION SALAD WITH MIXED GREENS

Winter is citrus season, so enjoy the fruits of winter by serving a variety of fresh citrus during the holidays. This salad combines the beautiful colors and lively flavors of oranges and red onions with a celery seed dressing.

DRESSING

$\frac{1}{2}$ cup peanut oil or salad oil

$\frac{1}{4}$ cup orange juice

4 teaspoons lemon juice

1$\frac{1}{2}$ teaspoons sugar

1 teaspoon celery seed

Dash salt

SALAD

5 cups crisp mixed greens (Romaine, red-leaf, and Boston lettuces) torn into bite-size pieces

1 head Belgian endive, sliced crosswise and separated

3 large oranges, peeled (remove all white), seeded, and sectioned

$\frac{2}{3}$ cup coarsely chopped red onions

Chives (optional)

TO MAKE THE DRESSING: Combine the oil, orange juice, lemon juice, sugar, celery seed, and salt in a screw-top jar; cover tightly and shake well. Set aside or refrigerate for up to 24 hours.

TO MAKE THE SALAD: In a large bowl, toss together the mixed greens and endive. Divide the greens among chilled salad plates and arrange the orange sections and onions on top of each portion of greens. Garnish with chives, if using. Pour about 2 tablespoons of the dressing on each salad and serve immediately.

Makes 6 servings.

CITRUS SALAD

This unusual salad is tasty and refreshing—and you make it a day before serving. Serve the salad with ham, lamb shish-kebab, or baked fish or chicken.

3 large oranges, peeled and sectioned

1 large pink grapefruit, peeled and sectioned

2 tablespoons sliced green onion

1 tablespoon snipped fresh mint

$\frac{1}{4}$ cup olive oil

2 tablespoons sugar

1 teaspoon finely shredded lemon peel

1 tablespoon lemon juice

$\frac{1}{4}$ teaspoon salt

4 cups shredded Romaine lettuce

Place the orange and grapefruit sections, onion, and mint in a medium bowl. In a screw-top jar, combine the oil, sugar, lemon peel, lemon juice, and salt. Cover and shake well. Pour over the fruit mixture and toss gently. Cover and refrigerate 12 to 24 hours.

At serving time, put the Romaine in a large salad bowl, top with the fruit mixture, and toss lightly. Serve immediately.

Makes 6 to 8 servings.

CHAPTER  4

Breads for Meals and Snacks

FRESH, WARM BREAD IS WON-
DERFUL ANYTIME AND IS ESPE-
CIALLY INVITING DURING THE
HOLIDAYS. THE QUICK-TO-MAKE
BREADS IN THIS CHAPTER ARE
EASY ON THE COOK AND ARE
WELCOME BY FAMILY AND GUESTS.
A LOAF OR TWO MAKES A GREAT
BREAD-AND-BUTTER GIFT TOO.

THE BREADS ALSO FREEZE
WELL FOR UP TO THREE MONTHS.
JUST LET THE BAKED BREAD
COOL COMPLETELY, THEN WRAP
IT WELL IN MOISTURE- AND
VAPOR-PROOF FREEZER PAPER
OR FOIL. DEFROST THE BREAD IN
THE WRAPPER, THEN HEAT IT
BEFORE SERVING, IF YOU LIKE.

EASY WHOLE-WHEAT BREAD

This no-knead, yeast bread is moist, rich-tasting, and nutritious with all the goodness of whole wheat and honey.

3¼ cups whole-wheat flour, divided
1 package of active dry yeast
1 teaspoon salt
1¼ cups warm water (120° to 130°F)
2 tablespoons cooking oil
2 tablespoons honey

Grease an 8" x 4" x 2" loaf pan and set aside. In a large mixer bowl, combine 1½ cups of the flour, yeast, and salt. Add the water, oil, and honey. Beat with an electric mixer on low to medium speed for 30 seconds, scraping the sides of the bowl. Beat on high speed for 3 minutes more. Using a wooden spoon, stir in the remaining flour. Spread the dough evenly in the prepared loaf pan, cover lightly, and set aside in a warm, draft-free place to rise until nearly double (about 45 minutes).

Preheat the oven to 375°F. Bake for 40 to 45 minutes, or until the bread sounds hollow when tapped. Remove the bread from the pan and cool on a wire rack before slicing.

Makes 1 loaf.

■ *Easy Whole-Wheat Bread*

BIG, WARM FLOUR TORTILLAS

Serve these chewy, plate-size breads from a basket with a Mexican meal. They're also great baked till crisp in the oven (375°F for 5 minutes) and spread with refried beans, then topped with cheese, guacamole, chopped tomatoes, and shredded lettuce. Or, spread them with pizza sauce, top with mozzarella cheese, and bake (375°F for 5 minutes) until the cheese melts.

1½ cups all-purpose or bread flour
1 teaspoon baking powder
½ teaspoon salt
2 tablespoons shortening
½ cup warm water

In a large mixing bowl, stir together the flour, baking powder, and salt. With a pastry blender or two knives, cut the shortening into the flour until the mixture resembles cornmeal. Add the water and mix until blended. Turn the dough out onto a lightly floured surface and knead for 5 minutes, adding just enough flour so the dough doesn't stick to your hands. Cover the dough and let it rest for at least 1 hour and up to 3 hours. (This will let the dough "relax" so it is less elastic and easier to form.)

Heat a large, heavy griddle or skillet on the stovetop over medium heat. Meanwhile, cut the dough into 6 pieces and roll each piece into a ball. On a lightly floured surface, flatten and roll out each ball into a thin circle 8 to 10 inches in diameter. Cook each tortilla on the ungreased griddle or skillet for 2 to 3 minutes, or until the surface is speckled with brown spots, turning once. As you take the tortillas off the griddle, stack them on a heat-proof plate, cover with a damp towel, and keep warm. Serve immediately or allow them to cool completely, then wrap them in a plastic bag and store in the refrigerator for up to 24 hours. Or, wrap for freezing and freeze for up to 3 months.

Makes 6 tortillas.

HAM AND CHEESE BREAD

This hearty bread is a good choice to serve with eggs for breakfast, with a fresh fruit or green salad for lunch, or with stew for dinner.

2 cups all-purpose flour
1 tablespoon baking powder
2 teaspoons sugar
½ teaspoon salt
¼ teaspoon freshly ground black pepper
½ cup diced ham
4 ounces shredded sharp Cheddar cheese (1 cup)
½ cup chopped onion
3 tablespoons melted butter or margarine or cooking oil
1 egg
1 cup milk

Preheat oven to 350°F. Grease an 8" x 4" x 2" loaf pan and set aside. In a large mixing bowl, stir together the flour, baking powder, sugar, salt, and pepper. Mix in the ham and cheese. In a small skillet, cook the onion in the butter, margarine, or oil until tender but not brown; do not drain. In a small bowl, beat together the egg and milk; add the onion mixture. Pour into the dry ingredients and stir just enough to blend. Pour the batter into the prepared pan. Bake for 45 to 55 minutes, or until a toothpick inserted in the center comes out clean. Cool at least 1 hour. Serve warm. Store in refrigerator, then reheat or toast leftovers.

Makes 1 loaf.

■ *Ham and Cheese Bread*

BAKED RHODE ISLAND JONNYCAKE

Hailing from our smallest state, this cakelike cornbread has fans all over the country. Serve it buttered with meals or as a base for creamed foods or chili.

1 cup all-purpose flour
1 cup yellow or white cornmeal
1 tablespoon baking powder
1/2 teaspoon salt
1 egg, lightly beaten
1 1/3 cups milk
1/4 cup margarine or butter, melted
2 tablespoons molasses or dark corn syrup

Preheat the oven to 375°F. Grease an 8" x 8" x 2" baking pan. In a medium bowl, stir together the flour, cornmeal, baking powder, and salt. In a small bowl, mix together the egg, milk, margarine or butter, and molasses or corn syrup. Pour into the flour mixture and stir just until mixed. Pour the batter into the prepared pan and bake 25 to 30 minutes, or until it is pale gold and springy to the touch. Turn the bread out onto a wire rack and let cool for 2 minutes, then turn upright and cut into 16 squares. Serve hot.

Makes 1 loaf.

PUMPERNICKEL MUFFINS

These versatile muffins can do double-duty: for a savory bread use caraway seeds, or for a sweeter version stir in raisins.

1 tablespoon caraway seeds or 1/2 cup raisins
2 tablespoons boiling water
1 cup all-purpose flour
3/4 cup rye flour
3 tablespoons brown sugar
1 tablespoon baking powder
1/2 teaspoon salt
1 egg
3/4 cup milk
1/4 cup cooking oil
1 tablespoon molasses

Preheat the oven to 400°F. Lightly grease 12 muffin cups or line them with paper bake cups. In a small bowl, soak the caraway seeds or the raisins in the boiling water for 20 minutes; do not drain. (If using raisins, stir them occasionally.) In a medium mixing bowl, stir together the flours, brown sugar, baking powder, and salt. In another bowl, mix the egg, milk, oil, and molasses; stir in the caraway seeds or raisins (with the soaking water). Make a well in the center of the dry ingredients and pour the liquids into the well. Stir quickly and lightly just until mixed—the batter should be lumpy. Spoon the batter into the prepared muffin cups, filling each cup two-thirds full. Bake 20 minutes, or until lightly browned. Serve warm.

Makes 12 muffins.

■ *Baked Rhode Island Jonnycake (left);*
Pumpernickel Muffins (right)

CHAPTER 5

Irresistible Holiday Desserts

A GREAT WAY TO ENTERTAIN
DURING THE HOLIDAYS IS WITH A
STUNNING BUFFET CROWDED
WITH A VARIETY OF SWEETS. AT
A BUFFET, MAKE SERVING SIM-
PLER FOR GUESTS BY CHOOSING
ITEMS THAT ARE PRE-PORTIONED,

OR SLICE CAKES AND PIES SO
YOUR GUESTS CAN PICK UP A
SINGLE SERVING. ALSO, BE SURE
TO PROVIDE A TREAT OR TWO FOR
GUESTS AND FAMILY WHO PRE-
FER A LIGHTER DESSERT, SUCH
AS THE APPLE DESSERT.

APPLE-RAISIN BARS

These chewy bars are just as delicious served on crystal plates with coffee as they are as an after-school snack with milk.

½ cup shortening
1 cup sugar
3 eggs
3 tablespoons milk
2 cups all-purpose flour
1 teaspoon baking powder
1 teaspoon ground cinnamon
½ teaspoon salt
½ teaspoon ground nutmeg
¼ teaspoon baking soda
¼ teaspoon ground cloves
1½ cups finely chopped, peeled apples
1 cup dark or golden raisins
Cream Cheese Frosting (recipe follows)
½ cup chopped pecans or walnuts

Preheat the oven to 350°F. Grease a 15" x 10" x 1" baking pan. In a large bowl, beat the shortening and sugar with an electric mixer until light. Add the eggs, 1 at a time, beating well after each addition. Stir in the milk. In a medium bowl, stir together the flour, baking powder, cinnamon, salt, nutmeg, baking soda, and cloves. Gradually add to the sugar mixture, beating at low speed just until combined. Fold in the apples and raisins. Spread the batter into the prepared pan. Bake for 25 minutes, or until a toothpick inserted in the center comes out clean. Cool on a wire rack.

Frost the cake, then sprinkle the nuts on top. Cut into 2" x 1½" bars. Store, covered, in the refrigerator.

Makes 50 bars.

CREAM CHEESE FROSTING

2 packages (3 ounces each) cream cheese, softened
1 teaspoon vanilla
3 cups sifted powdered sugar

In a medium bowl, beat the cream cheese and vanilla with an electric mixer until light. Gradually add the sugar at low speed; beat at medium speed until smooth and fluffy.

Makes about 2 cups.

VERY MOIST GINGERBREAD

Warm Christmas memories are made of gingerbread. This is an especially moist, spicy dessert. Serve it with a smooth, tangy lemon sauce after family dinners or when friends drop by.

1 cup dark molasses
1 cup firmly packed brown sugar
1 cup butter or margarine
2 eggs, lightly beaten
2¾ cups all-purpose flour
1 tablespoon ground cinnamon
2 teaspoons baking soda
2 teaspoons ground ginger
1 teaspoon ground nutmeg
½ teaspoon salt
1¼ cups milk
Lemon Sauce (recipe follows)

Preheat the oven to 350°F. Grease well and flour two 9" x 9" x 2" or two 8" x 8" x 2" baking pans; set aside. In a medium saucepan, heat the molasses, brown sugar, and butter or

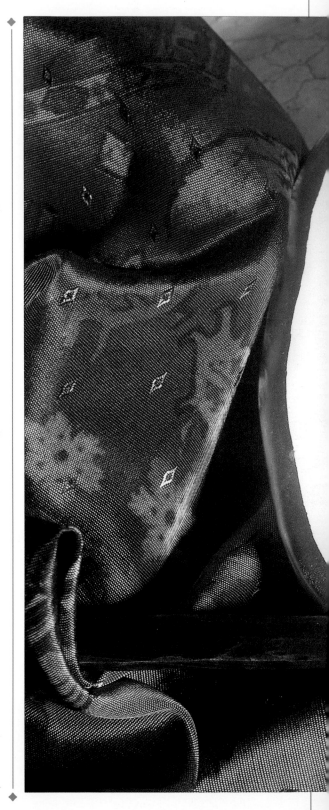

■ *Very Moist Gingerbread*

margarine over low heat, stirring constantly, just until the sugar and butter are melted. Remove from the heat; allow to cool for 10 minutes, then stir in the eggs.

In a large bowl, stir together the flour, cinnamon, baking soda, ginger, nutmeg, and salt. Stir the warm molasses mixture into the flour mixture; add the milk and mix together well. Pour the batter into the prepared pans and bake for 25 to 30 minutes or until a toothpick inserted in the center comes out clean. Cool slightly, then cut into squares. Serve warm with Lemon Sauce.

Makes 16 to 18 servings.

LEMON SAUCE

1 cup sugar
3 tablespoons cornstarch
1½ cups water
¼ cup butter or margarine
2 teaspoons finely shredded lemon peel
⅓ cup lemon juice

In a medium saucepan, stir together the sugar and cornstarch. Add the water and cook and stir over medium heat until thickened and bubbly; cook and stir 2 minutes more. Stir in the butter or margarine, lemon peel, and lemon juice. Serve hot.

Makes about 2¼ cups.

▪ *Cranberry-Berry Trifle (right)*

PUMPKIN-PECAN PIE

A crunchy pecan crust tops this smooth, creamy pumpkin pie—just the thing to serve after a special holiday meal.

Topping
½ cup firmly packed brown sugar
½ teaspoon ground cinnamon
⅓ cup margarine or butter
1 cup coarsely chopped pecans

Pie
3 eggs
1 can (16 ounces) pumpkin
1 can (12 ounces) evaporated milk
½ cup firmly packed brown sugar
1 tablespoon molasses
1 teaspoon ground cinnamon
1 teaspoon ground ginger
½ teaspoon ground allspice
¼ teaspoon ground cloves
¼ teaspoon salt
1 9-inch unbaked single-crust pie shell

To make the topping: In a small bowl, mix together the brown sugar and the cinnamon; with a fork or pastry blender, cut in the margarine or butter until the mixture is crumbly. Stir in the pecans and set aside.

To make the pie: Preheat the oven to 375°F. In a large bowl, whisk together the eggs, pumpkin, milk, brown sugar, molasses, cinnamon, ginger, allspice, cloves, and salt until smooth. Because the pie shell will be full and difficult to move without spilling, place the pie shell near the oven, then pour the filling into the shell; sprinkle the topping mixture evenly over the pumpkin. To prevent overbrowning, cover the edge of the pie with

foil. Carefully place the pie in the oven. Bake 25 minutes, remove the foil, then bake an additional 25 minutes, or until the crust is brown and a knife inserted near the center comes out clean. Cool to room temperature before serving. Store in the refrigerator.

Makes 6 to 8 servings.

CRANBERRY-BERRY TRIFLE

What a combination of flavors, textures, and colors! Tart cranberry sauce, sweet wine, cake, and custard come together for a sensational holiday dessert. For visual impact, layer the ingredients in a clear glass bowl.

1 package (4-serving-size) regular vanilla pudding mix
1½ cups milk
1 can (16 ounces) whole cranberry sauce
¾ cup strawberry jam
1 small (8" x 4") pound cake, cut into ¼-inch slices
¼ cup Marsala or other sweet wine
1 cup whipping cream
2 tablespoons sugar
Green and red candied cherries (optional)

Prepare the pudding according to package directions, using only 1½ cups milk. Cover surface with plastic wrap and set aside to cool.

In a small bowl, stir together the cranberry sauce and jam. Spread about ½ cup of the cranberry mixture onto half of the cake slices, then top with the plain cake slices. Cut each "sandwich" in half lengthwise. Pack the bars into a 2-quart square baking dish or clear glass bowl. Prick the cake all over with a skewer

or meat fork; sprinkle the cake with the wine. Spread with the remaining cranberry mixture, then with the cooled vanilla pudding. Cover and chill for 2 to 3 hours.

About 15 minutes before serving, place the whipping cream, a medium mixing bowl, and beaters in the freezer to chill. Shortly before serving, whip the cream with the sugar until soft peaks form. Frost the cold trifle with the whipped cream. Decorate with the cherries, if using.

Makes 9 servings.

APPLE DESSERT

This sweet, custardy dessert has 232 calories per serving.

1 can (8½ ounces) unsweetened applesauce
1 teaspoon ground cinnamon
4 eggs, beaten
1 can (12 ounces) evaporated skim milk
**½ cup frozen apple juice concentrate,
 thawed**
3 cups dry bread cubes
1 medium apple, peeled, cored, and chopped
**Thin slices of apple and cinnamon sticks
 (optional)**

Preheat the oven to 350°F. In a large bowl, mix together the applesauce and cinnamon. Stir in the eggs, milk, and juice concentrate. Fold in the bread cubes and chopped apple. Pour into a 2-quart square baking dish. Place the dish in a large metal baking pan; pour boiling water into the larger pan to a 1-inch depth. Carefully transfer to the oven. Bake, uncovered, for 30 to 35 minutes, or until a knife inserted in the center comes out clean.

Cool slightly and serve warm. Garnish with apple slices and cinnamon sticks, if using.

Makes 6 servings.

BANANAS FASTER

Based on elegant Bananas Foster, this dessert is a bit easier to make because the bananas are baked instead of cooked on the stovetop, so they require less watching. It is, however, just as impressive to serve. This recipe can be successfully doubled.

**4 bananas, peeled and cut on the diagonal
 into quarters**
¼ cup honey
¼ cup light rum
1 tablespoon butter or margarine, melted
1 tablespoon orange juice
¼ cup chopped pecans
4 scoops vanilla ice cream

Preheat the oven to 375°F. Place the bananas in a 2-quart square baking dish. In a small bowl, combine the honey, rum, butter or margarine, and orange juice. Pour the mixture over the bananas and sprinkle with the pecans. Bake for 12 to 15 minutes, or until the bananas are heated through.

Place a scoop of ice cream into 4 serving dishes. Portion 4 banana quarters and sauce over each serving of ice cream.

Makes 4 servings.

▪ *Apple Dessert (left); Bananas Faster (above)*

ORANGE FLANS

A variation of the classic Spanish custard, these flans are a smooth, cool finish to a dinner or a brunch.

1¼ cups sugar, divided
2 eggs
2 egg yolks
Dash of salt
2 cups half-and-half or light cream
2 tablespoons orange marmalade (cut up any large pieces)
Mint leaves and orange peel strips (optional)

Place 1 cup sugar in a medium skillet over medium-high heat. Stirring constantly, heat the sugar until it begins to melt, shaking the skillet occasionally to heat the sugar evenly. Reduce the heat to medium, and cook until the sugar is melted and turns *light* amber-brown (about 5 minutes more). Stir as necessary after sugar begins to melt. Immediately remove it from the heat. (If the sugar gets too brown, it will be bitter.) Using potholders to hold the cups and working quickly, pour the hot caramelized sugar into six 6-ounce custard cups, using a circular motion and allowing the liquid to run down the inside of the cups—it will harden as it cools. Set the custard cups aside.

Preheat the oven to 325°F. In a medium bowl, lightly mix the eggs, egg yolks, ¼ cup sugar, and salt. Gradually pour in the cream and marmalade, and stir thoroughly, but do not overmix. Pour the mixture into the prepared custard cups. Place the cups in a large shallow baking pan and pour in hot water to a 1-inch depth. Bake 35 to 45 minutes, or until a knife inserted near the center comes out clean.

Remove the custard from the water bath and cool. Cover with plastic wrap and chill in the refrigerator for at least 2 hours and up to 24 hours.

To serve, run a knife around the edge of each custard, place a rimmed plate or dessert bowl over the custard, and quickly invert the custard and plate together. Lift the custard cup off the custard. The caramelized sugar will make a sauce. Garnish the flans with mint and orange peel, if using.

Makes 6 servings.

TRIPLE-CHOCOLATE CHEESECAKE

This smooth chocolate cheesecake is based on a recipe from the Wisconsin Milk Marketing Board. It's rich and decadent and looks wonderfully tempting on a dessert buffet table.

CRUST
1½ cups chocolate sandwich cookie crumbs (about 18 cookies)
2 tablespoons sugar
¼ cup butter or margarine, softened

FILLING
4 packages (8 ounces each) cream cheese, at room temperature
⅓ cup all-purpose flour
1 can (14 ounces) sweetened condensed milk
4 eggs
1 tablespoon vanilla
4 squares (1 ounce each) semisweet chocolate, melted and cooled

GLAZE
3 squares (1 ounce each) semisweet chocolate, coarsely chopped
⅓ cup whipping cream
Whipped cream and chocolate sprinkles (optional)

TO MAKE THE CRUST: Preheat the oven to 325°F. In a medium bowl, stir together the cookie crumbs, sugar, and butter or margarine. Press into the bottom of a 9-inch springform pan. Bake 10 minutes; set aside.

TO MAKE THE FILLING: In a large bowl, cream together the cream cheese and flour. Gradually add the milk, then add the eggs, 1 at a time, mixing well after each addition. Stir in the vanilla. Divide the batter in half and stir the melted chocolate into one half and pour it into the crust. Carefully pour in the remaining batter over the chocolate batter. Bake 50 to 55 minutes, or until the center appears nearly set when shaken. Cool on a wire rack for 1 hour. Run a knife around the edge of the cake to loosen.

TO MAKE THE GLAZE: In a small saucepan, heat the chocolate and whipping cream, stirring until the chocolate is melted and mixture is smooth. Spread over the slightly cool cheesecake. Refrigerate for at least 6 hours or up to 24 hours before serving. Remove the sides of the springform pan. Garnish with whipped cream and sprinkles, if using, before serving.

Makes 12 servings.

▪ *Orange Flans (left)*

RICOTTA CHRISTMAS TART

Flecked with citron and nuts, this Italian-style cheesecake is wonderful any time of the year. The tart can be frozen after it is chilled—just wrap very well in foil, then freeze for up to one month. Defrost, still wrapped, at room temperature for three hours.

CRUST

2 cups all-purpose flour

1 teaspoon baking powder

1/4 teaspoon salt

3/4 cup butter or margarine, softened

2 tablespoons brandy or apple juice

3 to 4 tablespoons water

FILLING

24 ounces ricotta cheese, at room temperature

3 tablespoons toasted pine nuts

2 tablespoons chopped toasted almonds

2 tablespoons diced candied citron

1 tablespoon all-purpose flour

4 eggs

1 cup sugar

1 1/2 teaspoons vanilla

Almonds, candied cherries, and powdered sugar (optional)

TO MAKE THE CRUST: In a large bowl, mix the flour, baking powder, and salt. With a pastry blender, cut in the butter or margarine until the mixture is crumbly (like small peas). Add the brandy or juice and stir in enough water just until dough holds together. Cover and chill for 1 hour.

Remove one-third of the dough and return it to the refrigerator. Roll out remaining two-thirds of dough about 1/8-inch thick and transfer it to a 10-inch pie plate.

TO MAKE THE FILLING: Preheat the oven to 375°F. In a large bowl, mix the ricotta cheese, pine nuts, almonds, citron, and flour. In another bowl, beat the eggs until light and lemon-colored (about 5 minutes); gradually beat in the sugar; add the vanilla. Stir the egg mixture into the cheese mixture. Pour into the crust.

Roll the remaining pastry 1/8-inch thick and cut it into strips about 1/2- to 3/4-inch wide. Arrange lattice-style on top of pie. Trim the edges of the pastry to 1/2 inch, then turn the overhang under the pastry and press with a fork or with your fingers.

Bake for 45 minutes, or until firm. Cool on a wire rack for 1 hour. Refrigerate for at least 4 hours or up to 24 hours. Just before serving, decorate with almonds and candied cherries, then sprinkle with powdered sugar, if using. Let stand 30 minutes before serving.

Makes 10 servings.

DEEP CHOCOLATE APPLESAUCE CAKE

Applesauce gives this chocolate cake added body and moistness. Serve it with a scoop of vanilla ice cream or a dollop of whipped cream.

6 ounces semisweet chocolate

1 cup chocolate syrup

1 teaspoon vanilla

1/2 teaspoon almond extract (optional)

1 cup butter or margarine, softened

1 1/3 cups sugar

4 eggs

2 1/2 cups all-purpose flour

1/2 teaspoon baking soda

1 1/2 cups unsweetened applesauce

1 cup chopped walnuts (optional)

Sifted powdered sugar (optional)

Preheat the oven to 325°F. Grease and flour a 10-inch plain or fluted tube pan; set aside.

In a saucepan over very low heat, or in a microwave oven, melt the chocolate. Stir in the chocolate syrup, vanilla, and almond extract, if using. Set aside to cool.

In a large bowl, beat the butter or margarine with an electric mixer at medium speed until light; gradually beat in the sugar until fluffy. Add the eggs, 1 at a time, beating well (1 minute) after each addition. At low speed, beat in the cooled chocolate mixture.

Stir together the flour and baking soda. Add to the chocolate mixture alternately with the applesauce, beginning and ending with the flour and beating at low speed just until combined. Fold in the walnuts, if using. Pour the batter into the prepared pan and bake about 1 1/2 hours, or until a toothpick inserted in the center comes out clean.

Cool the pan on a wire rack for 15 minutes. Turn out of the pan and cool thoroughly. Sprinkle the top with powdered sugar, if using.

Makes 16 servings.

▪ *Ricotta Christmas Tart*

Jars Filled with Cookies and Candies

SWEET, COLORFUL COOKIES
AND CANDIES ARE SPECIAL
TREATS DURING THE CHRISTMAS
SEASON. SHARE THE JOY OF THE
SEASON BY FILLING A JAR WITH
SPICY JAM THUMBPRINTS OR
CHOCOLATE BUTTER COOKIES
AND INVITE LITTLE FOLKS TO

TAKE A HANDFUL OR TWO. MAIL
A BOX OF PATTY'S PEANUT
BUTTER BALLS TO FAR-OFF LOVED
ONES. AND STOCK A SUPPLY OF
STUFFED DRIED FRUIT FOR
FRIENDS WHO DROP BY FOR A
GLASS OF HOLIDAY CHEER AND A
CHRISTMAS NIBBLE.

SPICY JAM THUMBPRINTS

Children enjoy poking their little thumbs into the dough, then filling the holes with shiny red jam. (It's kind of fun for grown-ups, too.)

1 cup butter or margarine, softened
1½ cups firmly packed light brown sugar
1 egg
½ cup dairy sour cream, at room temperature
4 cups all-purpose flour
1 teaspoon ground cinnamon
½ teaspoon baking soda
½ teaspoon salt
About ½ cup strawberry or seedless red raspberry jam

Preheat the oven to 400°F. In a large bowl, beat together the butter or margarine and the sugar; add the egg and sour cream and beat until light. In another bowl, stir together the flour, cinnamon, baking soda, and salt. Gradually stir the flour mixture into the creamed mixture, beating at low speed just until combined. Shape the dough into balls about 1 inch in diameter and place on an ungreased baking sheet. With your thumb, make an indention in the top of each cookie. Fill each recess with about ¼ teaspoon jam. Bake for 10 to 12 minutes, or until lightly browned.

Makes about 7 dozen.

CINNAMON STARS

These spicy butter cookies will simply melt in your mouth.

1¼ cups butter, softened
¾ cup powdered sugar
2½ cups all-purpose flour
2 teaspoons ground cinnamon
½ teaspoon ground nutmeg
1 teaspoon vanilla
Powdered sugar

In a large bowl, cream the butter. Gradually add ¾ cup powdered sugar and beat until light and fluffy. In another bowl, stir together the flour, cinnamon, and nutmeg. Add the dry ingredients to the creamed mixture. Stir in the vanilla and mix well. Divide into 4 portions. Cover and chill at least 1 hour.

Preheat the oven to 325°F. Roll out one portion of the dough at a time on a lightly floured surface to a ¼-inch thickness. Cut out with a 1- or 2-inch star-shaped cookie cutter, dipping the cutter in flour as needed to keep the dough from sticking. Place on an ungreased baking sheet and bake for 12 to 15 minutes for 1-inch cookies and 15 to 18 minutes for 2-inch cookies. Remove to a wire rack to cool. Sprinkle the cookies with powdered sugar. Store in an airtight container with waxed paper between each layer, if desired.

Makes about 5 to 10 dozen.

CHOCOLATE BUTTER COOKIES

These tasty little cookies will satisfy your "chocoholic" friends and family during the holiday season. Form them as you like—with a cookie press or roll them into balls—then decorate as you like.

¾ cup butter, softened
⅔ cup sugar
1 egg yolk
1 teaspoon vanilla or ¼ teaspoon almond extract
1½ cups all-purpose flour
3 tablespoons unsweetened cocoa powder

Preheat the oven to 375°F. In a large bowl, beat together the butter, sugar, egg yolk, and vanilla or almond extract with an electric mixer. In another bowl, mix together the flour and cocoa powder. Gradually stir into the creamed mixture and mix at low speed just until combined.

With a cookie gun or press, make Christmas tree, wreath, or ribbon shapes. Or, with your hands, shape into balls about 1-inch in diameter. Place on an ungreased baking sheet and bake 6 to 8 minutes for shapes or 8 to 10 minutes for balls, or until set. Remove to a wire rack and cool, then decorate as desired.

Makes about 3 dozen balls or about 4 dozen shapes.

■ *Cinnamon Stars*

FROSTED CRANBERRY DROP COOKIES

The tartness of fresh cranberries gives a little bite to these soft cookies.

COOKIES
1 cup sugar
½ cup shortening
2 eggs
½ cup orange juice
2½ cups all-purpose flour
1½ teaspoons baking powder
½ teaspoon salt
1 cup coarsely chopped cranberries
½ cup coarsely chopped walnuts
1 tablespoon finely shredded orange peel

FROSTING
2 tablespoons margarine or butter, softened
2 tablespoons orange juice
2 cups sifted powdered sugar

TO MAKE THE COOKIES: Preheat the oven to 375°F. Lightly grease a baking sheet. In a large bowl, cream together the sugar with the shortening until light. Add the eggs and beat until combined. Mix in the orange juice. In another bowl, stir together the flour, baking powder, and salt. Stir into the creamed mixture and mix just until combined. Stir in the cranberries, walnuts, and orange peel. Drop the dough by teaspoons onto the baking sheet. Space 2 inches apart. Bake 10 to 12 minutes, or until just beginning to brown. Remove to a wire rack to cool.

TO MAKE THE FROSTING: Mix together the margarine or butter, orange juice, and powdered sugar until smooth. Spread frosting on cooled cookies.

Makes about 4 dozen.

ALMOND MACAROONS

Keep these cookies on hand for guests who love moist almond cookies.

1 can (8 ounces) almond paste
3 egg whites
1 cup granulated sugar
½ cup sifted powdered sugar

Move an oven rack to the lowest position. Preheat the oven to 300°F. Line 2 baking sheets with parchment or plain brown paper. With a sharp knife or in a food processor, chop the almond paste to the consistency of coarse meal. Place the almond paste and egg whites in a large bowl and mix well. Stir in the granulated sugar, a little at a time, then stir in the powdered sugar until smooth.

Drop the cookies by teaspoons onto the baking sheet so cookies are about 1-inch in diameter, placing them about 2 inches apart. Bake on lowest oven rack about 15 minutes, or until just beginning to turn tan. Remove from the oven and let cool completely on paper. Let the cookies dry on wire racks for 1 hour before storing up to 2 days in an airtight container with waxed paper between the layers.

Makes about 6 dozen.

▪ *Clockwise from left: Almond Macaroons, Cinnamon Stars, and Spicy Jam Thumbprints*

CHARLESTON SWEET SESAME WAFERS

¾ cup sesame seeds
½ cup butter, softened
2 cups firmly packed brown sugar
1 egg
1 teaspoon vanilla
1 cup all-purpose flour
½ teaspoon baking powder
¼ teaspoon salt

Preheat the oven to 325°F. Spread the sesame seeds in a large shallow baking pan and toast about 10 minutes, stirring occasionally, until golden. Set aside to cool.

In a medium mixing bowl, beat the butter until light. Add the brown sugar and beat thoroughly. Mix in the egg and vanilla; beat well. In a small bowl, stir together the flour, baking powder, and salt. Add to the sugar mixture and beat with an electric mixer at low speed just until combined. Stir in the cooled sesame seeds.

Line a baking sheet with foil, then butter the foil. Drop by level teaspoons onto the prepared pan, about 3 inches apart (cookies will spread as they bake). Bake about 10 to 12 minutes, or until golden brown.

Makes about 8 dozen.

▪ *Patty's Peanut Butter Balls*

PATTY'S PEANUT BUTTER BALLS

Patricia Shelley Bushman makes and shares these tasty candies every Christmas—much to the delight of her friends! Once you've tried them, they'll become one of your holiday traditions, too.

3 cups (18 ounces) semisweet chocolate pieces
2 tablespoons shortening
1 jar (12 ounces) chunky peanut butter
1 package (16 ounces) powdered sugar, sifted
1½ cups graham cracker crumbs
1 cup sweetened shredded coconut
1 cup butter or margarine, melted

In the top of a double boiler or in a microwave oven, melt the chocolate and shortening together. Set aside and keep warm.

In a large bowl, mix together the peanut butter, powdered sugar, cracker crumbs, and coconut. Pour the butter or margarine over the peanut butter mixture and mix well. Shape into 1-inch balls. Use a fork to dip each candy into the chocolate, covering the candy completely. Allow the excess chocolate to drain off. Place on waxed paper and leave to dry and set about 4 hours.

Makes about 7 dozen.

STRAWBERRY JAM BITES

A layer of strawberry jam is enclosed between a delicate cookie crust and a sweet coconut topping. These little gems are too fragile to mail, but are beautiful and delicious as part of a holiday cookie tray or boxed and nestled in a gift basket.

CRUST
1½ cups all-purpose flour
3 tablespoons sugar
1 teaspoon baking powder
¼ teaspoon salt
½ cup butter or margarine
1 egg
3 tablespoons orange juice

TOPPING
2 eggs
1 cup sugar
¼ cup melted butter or margarine
2 teaspoons vanilla
2½ cups coconut

FILLING
¾ cup strawberry jam
½ teaspoon finely shredded orange peel

Preheat the oven to 350°F. Lightly grease a 13" x 9" x 2" baking pan; set aside.

TO MAKE THE CRUST: In a medium bowl, stir together the flour, sugar, baking powder, and salt. With a pastry blender or 2 forks, cut in the butter or margarine until crumbly. Add the egg and orange juice; mix well. Pat the crust mixture into the bottom of the prepared pan. Bake 15 minutes.

TO MAKE THE TOPPING: In a medium bowl, beat the eggs until thick and lemon-colored (about 5 minutes). Beat in the sugar, butter or margarine, and vanilla. Stir in the coconut.

TO MAKE THE FILLING: In a small bowl, mix the jam and orange peel together.

TO ASSEMBLE: Carefully spread the jam filling over the pre-baked crust; spoon on the coconut topping and spread evenly. Bake 20 minutes more, or until set. Cool completely before cutting into 1-inch squares.

Makes about 10 dozen.

STUFFED DRIED FRUIT

Have fun with these sophisticated goodies. Stuff a variety of dried fruits with one or more flavored fondant fillings and serve with drinks or coffee after dinner. Or, wrap them in a pretty box to give or mail as a gift.

2 pounds mixed dried fruit (dates, pears, apricots, figs, prunes, peaches)
2/3 cup sweetened condensed milk
1 teaspoon vanilla
4 cups sifted powdered sugar
1 cup coarsely chopped toasted pecans, almonds, or walnuts (optional)
Nut halves to top fondant (optional)

Find or make an opening (a slit) in each piece of fruit for filling.

In a large bowl, mix the milk and vanilla. Stir in the powdered sugar, about 1/2 cup at a time, stirring constantly. (You may have to knead the last of the sugar by hand.) Knead nuts into fondant, if using. Press the fondant into an ungreased 2-quart square baking dish, cover, and chill about 2 hours until set.

With a spoon, scoop out fondant and roll into 1-inch balls. Stuff balls into the fruit pieces, or place each ball between 2 small dried fruit halves (sandwich-style). If using, press a nut half into the top of each fondant ball.

Makes about 60 pieces.

VARIATIONS:
ORANGE-RUM: Use rum flavoring instead of vanilla and add 1/8 teaspoon orange extract and 1 teaspoon finely shredded orange peel.

MAPLE SUGAR: Use 1/2 teaspoon maple flavoring instead of vanilla. Roll the filled fruit in finely crushed maple sugar or granulated sugar.

MARZIPAN ALMONDS: Use almond extract instead of vanilla and add a small amount of brown paste food coloring to color the fondant a light almond-shell color. If you add nuts, use finely chopped almonds. Form the fondant balls in the shape of whole almonds, then place them between or stuff in the dried fruit.

SNOWBALLS: Roll the fondant balls in shredded coconut before filling the fruit.

PEANUT BUTTER–HONEY SLICES

Need to make a last-minute hostess gift or a quick addition to a cookie tray? These treats are a tasty solution.

3 cups fine graham cracker crumbs
2 cups nonfat dry milk powder
1 cup creamy peanut butter
2/3 cup honey
1/2 cup water
2 cups chopped unsalted peanuts or flaked coconut or 1 cup chocolate sprinkles

In a large bowl, stir together the cracker crumbs and dry milk. Add peanut butter, honey, and water; stir, then knead with your hands until thoroughly blended.

Form the mixture into 4 logs, each 9 inches long. Spread the peanuts, coconut, or sprinkles on waxed paper, then roll the logs in it. Wrap and chill 1 hour. Cut into 1/2-inch slices. (If desired, store the logs in the refrigerator and slice before serving.)

Makes 6 dozen.

▪ *Stuffed Dried Fruit*

SOURCES

Most of the supplies called for in the directions for the projects in this book are available in craft stores. If you have difficulty finding specific items, contact the manufacturer for a listing of suppliers in your area.

ACCENT PAINTS
300 East Main Street
Lake Zurich, IL 60047
(708) 540-1604

COATS & CLARK/ANCHOR (EMBROIDERY FLOSS)
Consumer Service Dept.
30 Patewood Drive
Greenville, SC 29615
(800) 648-1479

DELTA PAINTS
2550 Pellissier Place
Whittier, CA 90601
(800) 423-4135

FREUDENBERG NONWOVENS (PELLON)
20 Industrial Avenue
Chelmsford, MA 01824
(508) 454-0461

C.M. OFFRAY AND SON (RIBBONS)
Route 24
Chester, NJ 07930
(908) 879-4700

TULIP PAINTS
24 Prime Park Way
Natick, MA 01760
(508) 650-5400

DESIGNERS

Our special thanks to the following designers who contributed projects for this book:

KOLLATH/McCANN—Christmas Wreaths, page 16; Candlelight Collection, page 31; Gift Wrappings, page 62

GINGER HANSEN SHAFER—Glorious Garlands, page 21; Nature Ornaments, page 28; Stamp Art, page 48; Gifts for Gardeners, page 51; Celestial Sweatshirt, page 59

MIMI SHIMMIN—Victorian Moiré Ornaments, page 23; Gold Star Ornaments, page 25; Mini Stockings, page 35; Elegant Holiday Place Mats, page 38; Kitchen Swag and Wreath, page 44; Black and Gold Lace Sachets, page 56

JACKIE SMYTH—Pine Sachets, page 52; Appliquéd Sweatshirts, page 60

PROP CREDITS

WE ARE GRATEFUL TO THE FOLLOWING COMPANIES FOR THE LOAN OF MANY FINE ITEMS FOR USE IN THE FOOD PHOTOGRAPHY. THOSE ITEMS NOT INDIVIDUALLY LISTED WE OBTAINED PRIVATELY.

Page 129: silver demitasse cup, saucer, & spoon—Artfield & Craftsmen, Los Angeles, CA. **Page 74**: relish tray, bone china basket; **Page 76**: silver relish tray; **Page 92**: gold fruit tray; **Page 95**: all dinnerware; **Page 104**: blue & white striped dinnerware; **Page 108**: all plates—Cuthbertson Imports Inc., Norwalk, CT. **Page 85**: luncheon plate, soup bowl; **Page 96**: luncheon plate; **Page 99**: dinner plate; **Page 100**: plate; **Page 106**: dinner plate; **Page 117**: luncheon plate, cup & saucer; **Page 121**: plate, cup & saucer—Cyclamen Studio, Berkeley, CA. **Page 75**: silver tray; **Page 115**: copper trivet—Old Dutch International and Leber Ltd., New York, NY. **Page 82**: star napkin, moon napkin ring; **Page 86**: soup tureen, bowl, plate, candlesticks; **Page 91**: plates, candlesticks, wine glass, place mat, napkin ring; **Page 99**: stemware candle holder; **Page 104**: plates, glasses; **Page 105**: basket with mugs; **Page 108**: wooden pull toy; **Page 110**: salad bowl; **Page 115**: all dinnerware, bowl, plate, cup & saucer; **Page 116**: plates, mugs, basket; **Page 123**: candlesticks; **Page 126**: plate; **Page 129**: plate; **Page 136**: basket; **Page 139**: wine glasses—Pier One Imports, New York, NY.

INDEX